Spiritual Dynamite

Spiritual Dynamite

Ron Marr

📖 Whitaker House

SPIRITUAL DYNAMITE

For other resources, contact:
Pastor Ron Marr
ChristLife
Box 263
Niagara Falls, NY 14305
(716) 284-7625

ISBN: 0-88368-576-0
Printed in the United States of America
Copyright © 1999 by ChristLife, Inc.

Whitaker House
30 Hunt Valley Circle
New Kensington, PA 15068

Library of Congress Cataloging-in-Publication Data

Marr, Ron, 1933–
    Spiritual dynamite / Ron Marr.
        p.   cm.
    ISBN 0-88368-576-0 (paperback)
    1. Devotional calendars.   I. Title.
  BV4811.M327   1999
  242'.2—dc21   99-10075

1 2 3 4 5 6 7 8 9 10 11 12 13 / 10 09 08 07 06 05 04 03 02 01 00 99

Contents

Preface

Just to be willing, by God's enabling, to worship the Lord and rest in Him whatever the circumstances He is permitting at the moment—that's spiritual dynamite!

It may seem impossible to rest contentedly in God in the midst of physical or emotional pain, time pressures, the follies and foibles of people, our own foolishness and sin, religious persecution, or lack of enough money to pay the bills. But when we turn in simple worship to the God who is ENOUGH; when we don't have to fight it all through, figure it all out, or fix it all up; when His acceptance is enough; when we don't have to deserve His love; when it is enough just to be in Him—the dynamic works. Like Paul, we can be content, for he said, *"I have learned in whatever state I am, to be content"* (Phil. 4:11). No matter how crushing our own world has been, though nothing changes, everything changes. Instead of being victims, immediately we are victors.

I have divided this book into thirty-one chapters so that it can be used as a one-month daily devotional. During thirty-one days, you will have the opportunity of unlocking the secrets to having true peace and contentment in your life. But remember, I can't really teach you anything. I can give you the information, but to teach you is the work of the Holy Spirit. Let Him work.

GOD IS ENOUGH!

Not God and...but GOD!
God is enough. God alone.
If I have all else
my heart would desire,
and have not Him, I have nothing.
If I have Him and nothing more,
I have everything.
My heart must be convinced of this.
Only then can I live in peace.
Otherwise, there will always be
something else I need urgently,
desperately.
And this lack,
this urgent need of filling this lack,
will forever drive me to distraction
and destroy my rightful peace and rest,
my quietness and confidence in the Lord.
This doesn't mean I don't recognize
other things
that might be considered needs.
It's only that, while I may see them
as good or desirable
if within God's will and purpose for me,
I won't see them as ultimate needs,
because God, and God alone,
is my only ultimate need.
And what He gives me, in the way and
time He gives it, is fine with me.
For He alone is ultimately enough.

Enough for me.
Yes, I have what humans view
as responsibilities.
But only those that are God-given
are truly mine.
And they are not so much
responsibilities as opportunities.
Opportunities to serve and please
and give pleasure to the One
who is Himself all I need,
and is increasingly, by His grace,
all I want.

Chapter 1

GOD

As Much Yours in the Dark As in the Light!

*The LORD is my light and my salvation;
whom shall I fear? The LORD is the strength of my
life; of whom shall I be afraid? When the wicked came
against me to eat up my flesh, my enemies and foes,
they stumbled and fell. Though an army may encamp
against me, my heart shall not fear; though war
should rise against me, in this I will be confident.
One thing I have desired of the LORD, that will I seek:
that I may dwell in the house of the LORD all the days
of my life, to behold the beauty of the LORD,
and to inquire in His temple.*
—Psalm 27:1–4

Did you get the message of the huge word *GOD*? Is He big to you, overshadowing all else? Or do the problems and difficulties of life overshadow your God? As you respond to God's work within, it's really for you to determine which it will be.

Is your God the creator and sustainer of all things? If He is, surely He can care for His loved little one, no matter what the threat. Is He able to do *"exceedingly abundantly above all that* [you] *ask or think"* (Eph. 3:20)? Can He turn rock into flowing water (Exod. 17:6)? Does He give you the desires of your heart (Ps. 37:4)? If the answers are all yes, then why do you need to worry and fear?

Of course, if the desires of your heart are pride, pleasure, or popularity—or even if they're life's basic necessities, such as food, clothing, and heat—if your desires are the things of this world, there may come times when you don't get as much of them as you want.

God Must Be Enough

God Himself must be what you want. He Himself is enough.

Normally God supplies an adequate amount of what we consider to be the necessities of life. Often He supplies these in abundance, *"above all that we ask or think."* But if your eyes are on these things and not on Him, there's bound to come a time when you'll want to accuse Him of not keeping His commitments. Instead, rejoice when you're deprived of the pleasant things of this life. Rejoice that you're counted worthy to suffer with Him (Acts 5:41).

Would you be free from fear, even if a whole army were to oppose you, simply because the Lord is your light and salvation, the strength of your life (Ps. 27:1)? You can be, if you're equally willing either to let Him send a thousand angels to your rescue or to die in the service of the King of Kings.

What's our problem? Why are we afraid to die? Paul said that he was *"confident, yes, well pleased rather to be absent from the body and to be present with the Lord"* (2 Cor. 5:8). After all, to be present with the Lord is so much better. Isn't it? Well...ISN'T IT?

Our pain will always be greatest when we want what we want, when we act like selfish children. It will always be least when we're content to live peacefully at ease with God as our satisfaction, whatever the situation in which we find ourselves.

God fed His prophet through the ravens, who airlifted emergency provisions to him, and through the bottomless container of oil. (See 1 Kings 17:5–6, 10–16.) And He is perfectly capable of doing the same today. This He has proven to me over and over again for many years as I've been without any visible means of support.

Where Are You Looking?

If your eyes are on the means of support rather than the God who is Himself enough, you'll live in perpetual fear. Let your eyes be on God, nothing less! Our only security is in being certain of God's love for us and knowing that we have access into His comfort no matter what. Neither people nor things can be our security. They'll always let us down.

Even knowing this, surely we'll experience fear at the beginning of each new frightful experience. But we can turn from fear to trust and joy as surely as we have a God!

What a Story!

I think there's no better illustration of this in all of Scripture than the prophet Habakkuk's delightful turnabout from sheer terror to rest and rejoicing in the Lord while there was no improvement in his circumstances—no hope of improvement, but rather the contrary.

When God revealed to the prophet that His people were going to be devastated by the wicked Chaldeans, Habakkuk went into a fit of despair. He cried out, *"Why do You...hold Your tongue when the wicked devours a person more righteous than he?"* (Hab. 1:13). But God did not change His mind or recall the judgment.

God had told Habakkuk, *"Be utterly astounded! For I will work a work in your days which you would not believe"* (v. 5). It was to be a work of judgment, not of mercy. The day of mercy was past, and Habakkuk literally shook with fear. He said, *"When I heard, my body trembled; my lips quivered at the voice; rottenness entered my bones; and I trembled in myself"* (Hab. 3:16).

However, Habakkuk found his solution in God:

> *Though the fig tree may not blossom, nor fruit be on the vines; though the labor of the olive may fail, and the fields yield no food; though the flock may be cut off from the fold, and there be no herd in the stalls; **yet I will rejoice in the LORD, I will joy in the God of my salvation.** The LORD God is my strength; He will make my feet like deer's feet, and He will make me walk on my high hills.*
> *(Hab. 3:17–19, emphasis added)*

When his focus changed, so did his response. Both your focus and response can change, too.

Whether our deliverance is temporal and physical or eternal and spiritual, we can be confident that God will deliver us. He can! There's nothing too hard for Him. We never need to worry. We never need to doubt! He cares.

Now, I suggest that you get your Bible, turn to Luke 12:4–44, and read these wonderful verses. This may be the only passage I ask you to turn to in this entire book. It is a special passage to me because the Lord gave it to me before I graduated from Bible school. I memorized all of these verses, in addition to the other eighteen verses in Luke 12.

God knew that I would need His special provision all my life. I've never been able to rely on men for my supply, though to my shame I've often tried.

It must be all right with us if there's no source or resource to meet our need. God is all the source and resource we'll ever really need.

Let me share with you just two verses from Luke 12. May they be an incentive to you to read them all. May God be the joy of your heart as you read His promises.

> *Do not seek what you should eat or what you should drink, nor have an anxious mind....But seek the kingdom of God, and all these things shall be added to you.*   *(Luke 12:29, 31)*

Chapter 2

Living Happily

Rejoice in the Lord always.
Again I will say, rejoice!
—Philippians 4:4

Rejoice always.
—1 Thessalonians 5:16

If we were always happy, there'd be no need of this chapter. I want to convince you that you can be happy—that you can be happy no matter what is happening within and around you.

To the non-Christian, the very idea of this makes no sense at all. But for us as believers, continual happiness really, practically can be your experience and mine day by day. On the other hand, you can be continually unhappy no matter what is happening within and around you.

During one time with the Lord, I wrote,

Why am I not happy?
I'm imperfect.
I'm not getting enough accomplished.
I don't love God enough.
I'm uncertain about important things.

17

I'm sure I could have easily added to these. Instead I went on:

How I can be happy:
Get alone with the Lord.
Let these concerns all go to Him.
Worship God.
Rejoice in who He is.
Rejoice that He is mine, I am His.
Rejoice in God's total competence on my
behalf, that He is enough.

By the time I'd finished writing, the tears were streaming down my cheeks and wetting my clothing. I was entirely at peace in the Lord. My tensions, my reasons for being unhappy, had all disappeared!

It's easy to be unhappy, even in the best of circumstances. To be happy, we must turn to God.

During another morning time alone with God, I wrote,

You're God. By Your choice You are mine.
And in that I revel and rejoice.

If I look at myself or my temporal circumstances, I hurt and fear. Only in You can I revel and rejoice.

Thank You that You teach me this in new ways day by day. May it be not only in new words, but in new life dimensions.

Thank You that this is possible.

But can I really look catastrophe in the eye and rest contentedly in You at the same time? If I can, surely this is the peace that passes all understanding.

Just today, as I was hurting and frightened, anxious and overburdened, I wrote in my prayer diary, "I don't have to. I don't have to do anything but rest in You. What joy!"

Take Note!

We're genuinely happy to the extent to which

- we trust God because we see Him as entirely trustworthy.
- we have a good conscience in Him.
- we rest at peace in Him.
- we worship, praise, and thank God in a way that moves our focus from ourselves to Him.
- we're living comfortably at home in God regardless of what is happening within and around us.
- we're thus centered on God.

Not to Worry!

If you don't think you're learning to trust God, to have a good conscience in Him, to rest at peace in Him, to worship Him, to be comfortably at home in Him, to be centered on Him—if you don't think you ever will—don't worry about it at this point. Not at all.

If you're not happy in this way right now, I want to show you how you can be happy in this way—how this description of a happy person can be a description of you.

You Can Always Return to Joy

I'm not trying to kid you. Until we get to heaven, there will probably be a great many times when you'll be unhappy. But I want to reassure you that there's always the possibility of returning soon to that place of peace and joy where you're comfortably at home in God—that place of genuine happiness.

We know that *"the kingdom of God is not eating and drinking, but righteousness and peace and joy in the Holy Spirit"* (Rom. 14:17).

This book is dedicated to helping you learn to worship God, rest peacefully in Him, live comfortably at home in Him, and so live happily.

> *For we are the circumcision* [God's people], *who worship God in the Spirit, rejoice in Christ Jesus, and have no confidence in the flesh.* (Phil. 3:3)

Of course, the reason that we do not have joy may be a physical problem. Sometimes a chemical imbalance in our physical bodies produces mental and emotional distress that may not be entirely corrected by spiritual means. This is an important consideration to keep in mind.

Now Hear This!

Nothing in this book should make you anything other than happy in the long run. When I help you face temporal realities that you'd rather not face, my intention is to help you to be happier at length. When

I make the suggestion that you need to let God change you on the inside, it may briefly make you less happy. But His purpose is to help you ultimately to be happier.

I remember one time, in a prolonged prayer period, how God showed me my awful sinfulness. But I also recall actually reveling in the joy of knowing that He loved me enough to show me my sinful self!

May every challenge to positive change that the Lord puts before you increase your happiness as it increases your harmony with God. May every difficulty you face be an opportunity to turn to Him, release the difficulty to Him, and return to resting in Him and His peace and joy.

> *My brethren, count it all joy when you fall into various trials.*   *(James 1:2)*

> *I am filled with comfort. I am exceedingly joyful in all our tribulation.*   *(2 Cor. 7:4)*

> *These things we write to you that your joy may be **full**.*   *(1 John 1:4, emphasis added)*

What bliss!

Chapter 3

Heaven Help Us!

Blessed are the poor in spirit...those who mourn...the meek...those who hunger and thirst for righteousness...the merciful...the pure in heart...the peacemakers...those who are persecuted for righteousness' sake....Blessed are you when they revile and persecute you, and say all kinds of evil against you falsely for My sake. Rejoice and be exceedingly glad, for great is your reward in heaven.
—Matthew 5:3–12

No matter what suggestions I make to help you be happy and healthy even if your world is falling apart, they'll mean little or nothing to you unless they become down-to-earth and practical to you personally. No matter how helpful they might seem, you have to actually see them working for you in everyday life.

Ultimately, only God can make possible the changes that need to be made in your life, as well as in mine.

One of the dear friends whom I know only by mail and phone was told often how she could return to trusting and resting in the Lord. In fact, she heard this so often that she came to the place where she just wanted to be delivered from her constant advisors.

And she didn't want any counsel from me at that point either. She was sick and tired of easy answers. She just wanted to be left alone.

The fact is, there are no easy answers. This isn't because what we need to know and do is hard to understand or perform, but because we don't want to do it. Our "wanter" is weak.

Our "Wanter" Is Weak, but Our Pain Is Our Gain!

Why is our "wanter" weak? The reason, in part at least, is that we hate the hurt.

For years I've preached that rebellion, resistance, and resentment are our curse. For years I've preached that we have to let go and let God. I've preached that we must believe that, in all reality, God actually does work all things together for our ultimate good (Rom. 8:28). I've preached that we need to trust in the Lord no matter what. We need to rest in Him and His peace whatever our circumstances. We need to worship, love, and adore Him; to praise and give Him thanks; to let go of everything to Him; to be nothing so He can be everything to us; to let Him turn our attention from ourselves and from our problems to Him.

And so we must. But very often we just can't seem to act on our knowledge of all these things we "need to do." We can't accept the reality that, in fact, our pain really is our gain. The hurt is too great.

Our "wanter" is weak because we hate the hurt, but there's more to it than that.

I'm Not in Control

As I was at prayer another morning, I read Romans 8:18–39. Then I wrote what was on my heart:

I hate my uncertainties, incapacities, and imperfections. I'm scared because I can't control everything.

Actually, there's very little I really can control. And what if I could control everything? Left to myself, I'd wreck everything I sought to control! There's so little I really know, nothing I know perfectly. Left on my own, I'd make my choices on the basis of incomplete and faulty information or assumptions. I would too often have selfish rather than unselfish motives. Except by God's divine intervention, my love would never be complete, or even adequate.

We Were Made for Perfection

While it's true that I'm that imperfect, it's also true, on the other hand, that we were made for perfection. We'll never be totally at home until we're perfect, in a perfect environment, with a perfect God.

I'm often amazed that we Christians don't look forward to heaven with the excitement it deserves. One of the first things we should be doing each morning, and one of the last things we should be doing each night, is thanking the Lord for the perfections of His heaven that await us. O God, forgive us for being such creatures of this world and so little creatures of the world to come.

As His own, we are only strangers and pilgrims down here, as we see in the following Scripture passage:

> *For here we have no continuing city, but we seek the one to come. Therefore by Him let us continually offer the sacrifice of praise to God, that is, the fruit of our lips, giving thanks to His name.*   *(Heb. 13:14–15)*

Who Can Fix Our "Wanter"?

So, between now and then, we need someone who can fix our "wanter." We need someone who can heal our hurt; who can enable us to increasingly accept our uncertainties, incapacities, and imperfections; who can control everything from a position of perfect power, perfect knowledge, and perfect wisdom; who has no uncertainty, incapacity, or imperfection; and who loves us enough to never allow anything to touch us with permanent harm, only with eternal good.

We have that One.

But so very often we prefer to turn inward to ourselves and our hurts. So we're left nursing our hurts and our hates, our fears and our frustrations, our uncertainties, our incapacities, and our imperfections.

Incredibly, I know of one person in a hopeless situation who found himself "praying" at one point that God would take him out of this horror to hell. Idiotic! Unbelievable! Insane!

But having created his own private hell here and now by refusing to turn to the God who can change hell on earth to heaven on earth, he felt at home only in some kind of hell. Why, oh, why would he neglect his only hope, the God of hope, in favor of his own private hell?

Peace Where There Should Be None

The Lord has offered us in every circumstance the peace that passes all understanding (Phil. 4:7)— peace when everything around us says there shouldn't be, there just can't be, any peace.

But to get that peace, we have to get to God. In order to get to God, we have to get release from our bondage to ourselves and our circumstances. And often, it seems, we don't want to be released. We don't want to let go. We want to hold on tight.

Many times we sit down and say, "After all, I have every reason to be anxious (or worried, afraid, frustrated, depressed, angry, unforgiving, hateful, bitter, upset, hopeless). I have every right to feel exactly as I do, and I'm going to nurse my misery. I'm going to enjoy it to the full. Nobody's going to take it away from me!"

In the pages of this book, I suggest many ways of getting off this out-of-control merry-go-round that's in no way merry. But I've found that the simplest and most successful way is to worship God. Or sometimes it is just to become nothing before Him. Having nothing. Being nothing. Wanting nothing. Just Him. Just letting Him be everything. And this is, perhaps, the best of worship!

Let what He is simply invade and pervade your heart, your mind, your soul, your spirit, your whole life.

Spiritual Dynamite

Now, let me say that to know this truth is of no real value unless you put it into practice.

Learn to Worship God or to Just Cast Yourself on Him

I'll tell you much more about how to learn to worship God in ways that I trust you'll find beneficial. But perhaps you may be able to begin right now. Get into your quiet place, whether just in your spirit or in an actual place. There you may want to tell God just where you're at, what you're feeling—if you're afraid of Him, mad at Him, feeling undeserving, if you don't really want to come to Him at all, if your heart is full of fear or anxiety, if you'd really rather forget the whole thing.

But whatever else you do, however you may be feeling, if you can, just start worshiping the Lord. Praise Him. Thank Him. Love Him. Adore Him. Honor Him. Seek His face. Speak His characteristics or attributes back to Him. Rejoice in Him. Rest in Him. Wait on Him. Tell Him you have nothing and are nothing. Your interest is just Him. Be quiet before Him.

You may be able to do little of this. You may be too far gone. Then don't pretend things are any different than they are. Don't try to accomplish anything. Just fall into His arms of love as an undeserving, hurting, needy, incapable little child might do.

If you can't, don't be concerned about it. Just commit the matter to God, and quietly read on.

28

Chapter 4

Why Rest When You Can
Fret 'n Fume 'n Fuss?

*There remains therefore a rest for the people of God.
For he who has entered His rest has himself also
ceased from his works as God did from His.*
—Hebrews 4:9–10

There's a great truth much neglected by Christian people everywhere. Whenever I teach it, I am met by a "Yes, but...."

Now, what is it? It's this:

To Rest in the Lord Is the Great Secret of
Spiritual Living

"Yes, but isn't it my responsibility to pray, study my Bible, obey the Lord, and work for Him? I can't just rest, can I?"

"Yes, but what about Philippians 2:12, *'Work out your own salvation with fear and trembling'*?"

Yes, what about it indeed? What about the next verse, *"For it is God who works in you both to will and to do for His good pleasure"*?

29

Have you ever actually met anyone whose imbalance fell on the side of resting in the Lord too much, who trusted too much in God's working, too little in his own?

I haven't. That's just not our problem.

His Rest Is Ours

Jesus said,

Come to Me, all you who labor and are heavy laden, and I will give you rest. Take My yoke upon you and learn from Me, for I am gentle and lowly in heart, and you will find rest for your souls. For My yoke is easy and My burden is light. (Matt. 11:28–30)

When He called to Himself all who labor and are heavy laden, He called the whole human race. We all struggle and strive. We stretch and strain. We fuss 'n fume.

One of my most frequent types of calls in counseling is from those who are depressed. And most often, when I find someone who is in physical need, I find someone who is also stressed out, worried, troubled, and anxious. They may not admit their depression, but it really is there. However, Jesus promised that if we will just come to Him, He will give us rest.

How wonderfully inclusive. To everyone who comes to Him, He gives rest. Did you ever think of it this way? Everyone who comes to Him gets rest. Wow!

On the other hand, this surely doesn't seem to be the case, does it? What's wrong? Have almost all who claim to be born-again children of God by faith never really come to Jesus? Not necessarily.

Come, Not Once but Forever

It isn't enough to come to Jesus just for personal salvation from sin and the gift of eternal life. Of course, that is necessary. It's the beginning of your relationship with God. It's the start of getting rest and peace from God, the beginning of getting all good things from Him. But it is only the beginning.

Just as we must come to Him once, trustingly and expectantly, to receive His personal gift of salvation and eternal life, so we must come to Him again and again, trustingly and expectantly, for rest, peace, and every good and perfect gift that comes down from above (James 1:17).

Come in each circumstance, each need, each pain, each problem, each opportunity, each impossibility. When you come, come in quiet trust. Lay yourself down in His arms of love. Rest there.

If you can't come in quiet trust, that's fine, too. To come as one who is needy, anxious, frightened, depressed, lonely, weary, or heavy laden is okay. God always accepts us just as we are. But we mustn't be content to stay that way.

Look to Him as *"the God of all grace"* (1 Pet. 5:10). Quietly worship Him. Thank Him for who He is. Let Him turn your attention from yourself to Him. There's no rest in you. There's only turmoil.

But the wicked are like the troubled sea, when it cannot rest, whose waters cast up mire and dirt. "There is no peace," says my God, "for the wicked." *(Isa. 57:20–21)*

This is obviously a picture of the godless. But surely it is equally a picture of God's saints when they wickedly turn from Him and His rest and peace to rely on themselves. How many of us can give sad testimonial to this reality!

Our righteousness and our rest are never found in ourselves, only in Him. So let us come again and again to have our attention transferred from ourselves to Him, and to have our hopelessness and turmoil transformed into the hope, the rest, and the peace that are in Him.

Come and Stay

Better than constantly coming and going is coming to stay. *"Abide* [stay, remain, rest] *in Me, and I in you....For without Me you can do nothing"* (John 15:4–5).

What does abiding in Him entail? First, it entails a recognition of who our triune God is.

He is love (1 John 4:8).

He loves us.

He is absolutely trustworthy.

He never allows anything to come into our lives that is not for our eternal good as well as His eternal glory.

He is omnipotent, omniscient, omnipresent—all-powerful, all-knowing, always present with us.

He is infinitely perfect. He is perfectly infinite.

In spite of the presence and power of sin and Satan, in spite of man's freedom to choose even that which hurts and destroys, there's nothing that is outside of God's sovereign ability. (See Romans 8:28.) Now, I don't understand this, but I do believe it.

Abiding in Christ also entails a recognition of our place in Him. We are *"accepted in the Beloved"* (Eph. 1:6). His righteousness has been imputed to us, credited to our account. So positionally, though not in everyday practice, we are perfect in Him. We can stand confident of His acceptance, His love, His understanding care and compassion...not because of anything we have done or do, but because of what He has done for us.

I Am in Christ, Christ Is in Me

We are always in Him positionally, whether we feel it, whether we think it, whether we believe it or not. We are in Him; therefore, remaining in Him, we are in His rest. This is the position in which we belong.

Abiding in Christ entails accepting His place in us, too. He has promised never to leave us or forsake us (Heb. 13:5).

Now, we may think of this as meaning that He's like a friend who is alongside us. We think that there is some distance between us, even if it is just a little distance.

No, His presence is more than that. He's actually in us. *"Christ in you, the hope of glory"* (Col. 1:27).

He is in us as our very life. Colossians 3:4 says so: "[He] *is our life."* When we first came to Christ for personal salvation and received eternal, spiritual life, we didn't just get life as a thing. We got the Person, Jesus Christ, who is "the Life."

So we need to be ever learning to turn to our perfectly loving, perfectly capable God who lives in us. We need to always come to, and increasingly remain at rest in, the One who lives and resides in us as our very life.

Is Resting in Jesus an Option or a Necessity?

To rest in the Lord is the great secret of spiritual living.

Sound familiar? I used these same words at the beginning of this chapter, stating that it's a great truth much neglected by Christian people everywhere.

It seems almost impossible for us to believe that our very spiritual welfare, our Christian victory, our happiness in Christ, depends on our willingness to rest in the Lord. But it does. We would rather depend on our works, our ability to do, to accomplish, even to trust, than to rest in the Lord's ability to do for us. But our way, the way of works, can end only in spiritual failure and unhappiness. God's way, the way of submission and humility, the way of neediness and dependence on God, the way of rest and peace, will always end in spiritual victory and lasting joy.

Resting in the Lord works wonders in the most delightful, practical ways. One morning I just couldn't find the Lord at all. I was entirely "discombobulated." Suddenly I stopped striving, trying for anything. I relaxed, the tears flowed, and I was at peace in Jesus. What relief! What release! What joy!

Allow me to give you another example. When I first sat down to prepare a particular mailing, I just couldn't get a handle on it. Though I had previously prepared some notes, I couldn't get started.

I knew I had an option. I could try, or I could trust and rest. Deliberately, I leaned back in my chair and talked to the Lord about it. In a few minutes I was entirely at peace, drifting into sleep a little but still communing with Him. After a half hour or so, I awoke, turned to the Word, and in a few minutes was confident I knew what the Lord would have me share.

Oh, that I always turned so readily from my fussing to trusting and resting in the Lord!

Do you feel this way, too?

Chapter 5

Peace through Prayer

Continue earnestly in prayer, being vigilant
in it with thanksgiving.
—Colossians 4:2

And let the peace of God rule in your hearts, to which
also you were called in one body; and be thankful.
—Colossians 3:15

I have found it beneficial to record some of my prayers in a prayer diary. One of my prayer diary entries reads like this:

> There's constant tension in my life. It's fear-induced. I have neither right to this nor need of it. If I live in You and Your peace, in a constant inner awareness of Your all-sufficiency for all things, I need fear no failure, no lack, no inadequacy, no mistake, no attack from without, no responsibility, no need, nothing.
> NOTHING.
> God is enough.

I wrote that years ago. My prayer now is that the Lord will help me live out this truth day by day.

Now, Mark This! The Next Few Paragraphs Are the Key to the Spiritual Message of This Book.

Let me continue my quotation from my prayer diary:

I cannot strive and struggle and at the same time live in peace. I must not listen to others but to my God-sensitive heart and spirit. I must choose to live in peace based on an all-pervasive trust in You.

The biggest spiritual battle I fight, and the only one, I think, that really matters, is the battle to set all else aside in favor of trusting and resting in You as the God who is truly adequate for everything, all-sufficient always in all things to all men everywhere.

Our special battles against the world, the flesh, and the Devil are won right here.

I've determined to trust You completely hundreds of times over the years, only to be misled by my fleshly desires and what others teach. Help me never to be so misled again. Help it to be my one business night and day to live in peace in You in the inner awareness that You're always all-sufficient for all things, for both me and all for whom I pray.

Anything that limits or destroys my peace in the all-sufficient God must be counted a sin and an enemy.

Sometimes I must worship, praise, or thank You for who You are, or sit in silent adoration, before I can enter Your rest. Sometimes I'm helped by reading a writer of years gone by or my own writings. Often I tell You that nothing matters. Just You. You alone. You only. Other times, when You enable, just to turn toward You with a quiet spirit is enough.

Nothing Is More Important

My prayer diary entry continues:

Worship, praise, intercession, petition, thanksgiving, adoration, and expressed love all have their rightful place in our daily prayer times and in our entire lives. So do reading, studying, and understanding the Word, listening to You, submission, obedience, repentance, restitution, placing ourselves under the blood of Christ, and taking authority over sin and satanic forces of evil. But if these take precedence over living in peace and rest in our all-sufficient God, if they limit or prevent it, they must be temporarily set aside as impediments in the way of God's best.

To make this mindset operative throughout the day, I must slow down. Every time I find myself unnecessarily hurried, I need to recognize the hurry as the sin of not trusting You, as a sin against Your all-sufficiency, a sin against Your peace that passes all understanding. I must turn to You, look to You, the All-Sufficient One, slow down, and walk in quiet trust in You and Your all-sufficiency. It's not enough to do this occasionally. It's necessary to seek to do it always by Your enabling grace.

The Key!

*Not that I speak in regard to need, for I have
learned in whatever state I am, to be content: I
know how to be abased, and I know how to
abound. Everywhere and in all things I have
learned both to be full and to be hungry, both
to abound and to suffer need. I can do all
things through Christ who strengthens me.*
                                        (Phil. 4:11–13)

Here we have not just the fruit of walking with
God in rest, peace, joy, and liberty. Here we have the
key to walking with God in rest, peace, joy, and liberty! The key is to rest contentedly in Him. I praise
the Lord that He has made this real to me again and
again.

What a treasure!

What a relief!

I preach it. I teach it. I believe it with all my
heart. But how difficult it is to live it! Everything in
this life fights against it.

Now, once again, simply stated, what is this key?
It is just to be willing, by God's enabling, to rest contentedly in Him whatever the circumstances He is
permitting at this very moment.

It seems totally impossible to be content in God
in the midst of physical pain; emotional pain; time
pressures; physical deprivation; persecution; the follies and foibles of people; our own foolishness and
sin; our lack of knowledge, understanding, and ability; financial difficulties; lack of enough money to pay
the bills; even the lack of what we see as basic necessities of life. The very idea of being content in God in
these circumstances may strike you as foolish.

Content in Spite of Sin

So, difficult as it may be—almost impossible as it may be—at last we may begin to learn that God can be trusted with all of the circumstances of our lives. Also, we may start to understand that our responsibility to do something about our circumstances isn't nearly as important as our willingness to trust Him with them and live contentedly in Him in the midst of the worst of them.

But to live contentedly in Him in the midst of the mounting evidence of our constant sinfulness— we may be sure this is impossible! God couldn't permit it. Never. If He did, He'd be approving our sin. Right?

Wrong!

Grace or Works?

This thinking shows how much we depend on our own works for our relationship with God. It shows how little we understand that it's all by grace, not a bit by works. It shows how little we believe that the work of changing us into the image of God in our daily walk is all the work of God and His undeserved mercy, not the work of our own independent effort. Works won't cut it—no more for our sanctification than for our salvation; no more for the everyday victory over our sins than for the initial pardon of our sins.

And it shows how little importance we give to our place in Christ. It shows how little appreciation we have for the reality that we are *"accepted in the*

Beloved" (Eph. 1:6)—that through the finished work of Christ on the cross and His indwelling presence and power, we are always acceptable to God in spite of our sinfulness.

We can actually be content in the midst of our sinful failures. We can be content that God is forgiving us, cleansing us, owning us as His own, and changing us into His likeness as we're simply willing, by His grace, to rest in Him.

But How?

Most likely, there will be times when we aren't willing to rest in Him. And sometimes these times may be prolonged. But we must have this rest always before us as a goal. We must seek daily to learn more about resting in Him.

First, seek to come to a state of quiet rest in Him in your prayer time in the morning. Then, at every opportunity, and especially when you realize you're not resting in Him, look to Him. Tell Him, "Okay, Lord, I have nothing to offer You, nothing to ask of You. I come to You just for You."

If your heart won't accept this, try to get alone with Him until it will. Look not to the circumstances, but to the God who has permitted them and is working them together for your good (Rom. 8:28), however grievous they seem. Cast yourself on Him as your only hope. He is your rest, peace, joy, and liberty—ENOUGH for you no matter the situation in which you find yourself.

Worship Him. Give Him praise, honor, and glory for who He is. See Him as the God of peace. Recall

His promise to keep in perfect peace those whose minds are steadfastly focused on Him, because they trust Him (Isa. 26:3). Recall His commitment that His peace, which passes all understanding, will guard our hearts as we rejoice in Him and as we, in prayer, allow thanksgiving to replace our natural anxiety (Phil. 4:4–7). By His grace, rest contentedly in Him.

> *Let the peace of God rule in your hearts, to which also you were called in one body; and be thankful.* (Col. 3:15)

> *Rejoice in the Lord always. Again I will say, rejoice!...Be anxious for nothing, but in everything by prayer and supplication, with thanksgiving, let your requests be made known to God; and the peace of God, which surpasses all understanding, will guard your hearts and minds through Christ Jesus....Not that I speak in regard to need, for I have learned in whatever state I am, to be content.* (Phil. 4:4, 6–7, 11)

Chapter 6

Life Worth Living

All things work together for good to those who
love God, to those who are the called
according to His purpose.
—Romans 8:28

Resting contentedly in Jesus is not something that characterizes most Christians. It is anything but. To fret 'n fume 'n fuss is much more our lot. In this, as in too many other ways, we're little different from those who don't have a Savior.

What is our problem?

Why are we discontented?

Why are we dissatisfied with our spiritual lives?

Why are so many of us disappointed with the Lord's response to our concerns?

Why don't we get what we want out of our Christian lives?

Why aren't we happy, rejoicing in Christ?

Now, my friend, let us be real with ourselves and the Lord. I'm not suggesting that we should expect to live in some kind of flawlessness. I'm not suggesting that in this life we'll ever arrive at the place where we'll no longer fail God and have sad reason to regret our failures. Hardly! But I am suggesting that there's a life more satisfactory than most of us are living. And I've just told you what it is.

Rest Contentedly in God and His Will

What could be simpler than this?
Nothing.
Nothing...except that we just can't do it! It's absolutely impossible, even for converted children of God, to live restfully content in Him and His will unless the Lord Himself makes it possible. All of it is His doing. None of it is ours.

Where Does the Process Start?

The process starts where none of us want it to start. It starts with pain and suffering. And, as I've already pointed out, we flee from that as from the plague. But I've become convinced after reading the Word, experiencing life, and watching others, that there's no shortcut to godliness.

> [He] *chastened us...for our profit, that we may be partakers of His holiness. Now no chastening seems to be joyful for the present, but painful; nevertheless, afterward it yields the peaceable fruit of righteousness to those who have been trained by it.* (Heb. 12:10–11)

> *May the God of all grace, who called us to His eternal glory by Christ Jesus, after you have suffered a while, perfect, establish, strengthen, and settle you.* (1 Pet. 5:10)

To these I will add, as we move along, many other Scriptures that show us the vital role that suffering plays in our growth in the Lord.

If we won't accept God's use of suffering to bring us eternal benefit, we can't accept one of our favorite Scripture verses either, the one with which we opened this chapter, Romans 8:28. We can't really accept this verse, no matter how much we may pretend to.

What Will We Do about the Inescapable Suffering?

From infancy we've all suffered in this vale of tears, and so we shall until we join the Lord in our perfect eternal home. We can accept the pain and suffering as evidence of God's love and as His will for us, or we can fight them and Him to our eternal loss.

The problem is that we naturally fear and flee pain...and the God who permits it. Consequently, we find ourselves inadvertently in rebellion against God. Far from resting contentedly in His love and His will, which are expressed even in painful circumstances, we inwardly resent these circumstances. This attitude builds a wall of separation between us and the God we profess to love and serve.

Now, God in His infinite mercy and grace may break through that wall from time to time to reveal Himself and to do us good. But while that wall exists, there's no continuing intimacy in our relationship with God. We live in perpetual disappointment—sometimes well hidden, sometimes all too evident.

What Can We Do?

What we can't do is force ourselves to immediately start resting in God and His will for us, whatever it may include of pain and suffering. We just can't. It's of no use to try.

What we can do, if we want God's best for us, is to tell Him it's okay for Him to do whatever He needs to do, whether it's pleasant or unpleasant, to teach us to trustingly be content in Him in all things.

There's little danger of our being insincere in telling Him that. We'll not likely say it unless He has already substantially broken our stubborn wills. If we're unwilling to tell Him it's okay, and unwilling to give Him permission to use His own gracious means to bring us to the place where we're willing, we had better tear Romans 8:28 from our Bibles.

Perhaps the problem is that we're not willing to wait for the good He has promised. We would rather have our present pleasure with eternal loss than present pain with eternal gain. Now, are we quite sure we'll be glad a hundred million years from now that this was our decision?

Personal Experience

Do I know what I'm talking about?

Yes, I do. My wife and I suffered extreme financial distress for many years. Eventually we lost a publishing ministry that we had invested more than fifteen years into and had built up to nearly 100,000 paid subscribers.

Now my whole life is limited by my dear wife's illness with Parkinson's disease. Many nights I'm up with her several times, sometimes for an hour or more at a time. Sometimes she's had incredible physical pain. More often the pain is emotional. She never knows from minute to minute whether she will not be able to move her limbs or whether her body won't stop moving.

My wife, Ruthie, called to me a few minutes ago. As I hugged and comforted her, I thanked God for permitting the terrible distress she was experiencing right then. I asked Him to enable me to share more fully in her pain rather than trying to run away from it. Then I asked Him to care for her need. Does this mean that I perfectly practice what I preach about resting contentedly in the Lord, His will, and His love? Hardly! It means that God, in His undeserved mercy and grace, hasn't given up on patiently teaching this poor rebel to trust Him. For the little I have learned to practice, I give Him eternal praise.

Moreover, I revel in the assurance that all the pain is a small investment that will be multiplied and returned over and over in eternal blessings throughout the endless ages.

What Will You Do?

Won't you join me in learning to be content in God's love and His will, as evidenced in every circumstance He permits in your life, whether pleasant or unpleasant?

Can you imagine the fountain of living water that would overflow onto a sinning, hurting world to its eternal blessing if all God's people learned just to rest in Him?

Can you imagine the transformation of the saints—their newfound *"love, joy, peace, longsuffering, kindness, goodness, faithfulness, gentleness, self-control"* (Gal. 5:22–23)?

Can you imagine the lost sinners who would be swept into the fold?

Can you imagine the wonderful changes in society—the reduction of selfishness, anger, and hatred, and the increase of happiness and peace in this hurting world?

Well, first recognize this as a worthy goal: Rest contentedly in God and His will, which is evidenced by the circumstances He allows in your life. Second, remember that God is actually working every part of life's circumstances together for your eternal benefit (Rom. 8:28). Invite Him to do whatever He must to enable you to honestly ask Him to use His best tools, pleasant or unpleasant, to make it possible for you to rest in Him and His will. Then watch the wonder of His working, the mounting benefit for time and eternity, and the praise accruing to His worthy name.

Chapter 7

Shell-Shocked Christians

If God is for us, who can be against us?
He who did not spare His own Son, but delivered
Him up for us all, how shall He not with Him also
freely give us all things?
—Romans 8:31–32

It is good for me that I have been afflicted,
that I may learn Your statutes.
—Psalm 119:71

It is better to trust in the LORD than to put
confidence in man.
—Psalm 118:8

When we tell the Lord's people that their hope is just to rest in Jesus, many can't accept the simplicity of this statement. Many don't want to. They want to keep on trying to do something to deserve spiritual growth and victory—even after years of failure that is obvious to those around them, if not to themselves.

But there are others who want so badly to accept this truth. Some want it so badly that they actively work at finding a way to rest in Jesus. They gobble up all the books they can find that might help them. They gather information from whatever source.

While some make little progress in learning to walk with the Lord in rest and peace, others make good progress for a time, only to find after a while, to their great disappointment, the progress ends.

Why Such Difficulty?

Undoubtedly, there are many reasons for these difficulties, but one fact encompasses a great many of them: millions of God's people are victims of shell-shock!

There has been a great to-do over abusive homes and families. It's been all the rage to dig into your past and discover a history of abuse that is the cause of all your failure to cope adequately with life. And certainly, for many of us, the beginning of our shell-shocked state can be traced to our infancy, even if we had "good" parents.

As Romans 8:18–28 and other passages make clear, just living in this sinful world is a painful process. And it didn't stop being a painful process when we grew up and got out on our own. Now the abusers are our adult peers, life's difficult circumstances, illnesses, financial reverses, sorrow, death, perhaps even our children, and most certainly ourselves!

With each new difficulty that bombards us, we hurt more, and we react, as trauma victims will, by withdrawal. Instead of turning to God, we turn to television or some other sedative. The pain grows unbearable. We can hardly take any more.

Unrealistic Expectations

As Christians, we expect prayer to be a great source of comfort in such trials. But sometimes it is instead a great source of disappointment and pain. It contributes to our shell-shocked state. Why? Because we expect answers to prayer that we don't get. And we are disappointed. We are disillusioned. We are frightened. We are hurt.

We expect to get what we want from God without adequate concern for what God wants. We expect the Christian life to be easy, when Jesus' testimony and Paul's testimony is that it is hard, very hard indeed.

It's a shame, but it seems that a large portion of the church doesn't know how to read the Scriptures. The whole testimony of Scripture is that, for most people, life is very hard. Even the psalmist David, who is so often quoted to sustain a contrary viewpoint, was for much of his life a hated and hunted man.

When things got easier, David got in even worse trouble, becoming an adulterer and a murderer. God wouldn't even let him build Him a temple because he was a bloody man. (See 1 Chronicles 22:7–8.)

His son Solomon, who had things so easy, was the wisest of men. Still, he flagrantly disobeyed God in multiplying wives and in building an army of chariots on which he chose to depend, rather than on God. (See Deuteronomy 17:15–17.) He sowed the seeds of the destruction of the nation his father had built. And you can't believe for a moment that none of this cost him personal pain.

Unreal Assessment of Our
Rebelliousness and Sin

"The heart is deceitful above all things, and desperately wicked; who can know it?" (Jer. 17:9). Even if we could fathom the continuing evil of our redeemed hearts, we would rarely want to know it. Many of us prefer to see ourselves as fairly decent human beings made better by our conversion to Christ. Instead, we need to be willing to always see ourselves as deserving only hell.

As a result of our faulty assessment, we pridefully anticipate having a much easier time learning to walk with God in rest, peace, and joy than we do. We're disappointed, and often discouraged, by our failure to live in Christian victory as we've been taught we can and should. And, though we might never admit it, we tend to blame God for letting us down.

Inability of the Shell-Shocked

The truth of Romans 8:28 is lost on the victims of shell-shock. No matter how much we profess to believe that God is seeking to work all things together for our good, we really don't.

We can't trust God to work all things together for our good while, at the same time, we're blaming Him for letting us down. Nor can we withdraw into Jesus in rest, peace, and quiet trust. The trust just isn't there.

So what do we do? What we almost always do. We revert to some kind of works-righteousness. We condemn ourselves and say that we repent for not trusting God. We tell Him that we know He can be trusted and that we'll trust Him.

We may promise to spend more time alone with Him, expecting that to be the cure. But we may not find it to be so.

The Only Cure

The only way to see this hopeless situation begin to turn around is to start to live in present, practical God-consciousness. He alone is ever, always our only hope.

But if we can't withdraw into Jesus in rest, peace, and quiet trust, how can we live in present, practical God-consciousness?

Yes, spend more time alone with the Lord. But during that time, do whatever will help you to focus your attention on God and to take it off yourself, your difficulties, your needs, your pain, your worries. The only antidote to your hopeless self is your all-powerful God.

Chapter 8

Job's Story Is Our Story

Then the LORD answered Job..."Would you condemn Me that you may be justified?"
—Job 40:6, 8

Then Job answered the LORD..."I have heard of You by the hearing of the ear, but now my eye sees You. Therefore I abhor myself, and repent in dust and ashes."
—Job 42:1, 5–6

The lady on the other end of the phone line was, though I'd never seen her, a dear, dear friend who loved the Lord deeply and sincerely. She was suffering physically and emotionally. And, to some little extent at least, I was suffering with her.

I listened to her tale of woe. When at last I spoke up, it was to say, "For me to say anything or to give you any advice right now would be pure arrogance." From the other end came a loud "Amen."

She told me why. It was the story of Job and his comforters all over again! Christian friends, however well they meant, were only adding to her hurt. *They* knew why God's hand was heavy on her. *They* knew the way out. If only she'd listen to *them,* she'd be fine!

As I pointed her to Jesus, she told me that she accepted my intervention because she knew that I cared. But she didn't know that I wasn't giving her the bottom line as frankly as I wished I could.

I didn't want to pain her pointlessly. And she wasn't ready to hear that she was resisting God's hand, which was on her life for her own benefit. She didn't want me to tell her that she was rejecting with her heart what her head knew so well, that the pain she was experiencing was the very best God could give her at that moment. She didn't want to hear the truth that by responding this way, she was only increasing the hurt and reducing the blessing.

Yes, she was responding very much as Job did, and as people throughout the ages have done.

My heart ached for her. I felt so helpless.

It Wasn't All the Devil's Idea

It seemed that Job's awful trials were all the Devil's idea. But the truth is revealed in Job 42:11: *"They consoled him and comforted him for all the adversity that the LORD had brought upon him."* Job's circumstances truly were *"adversit*[ies]." However, though the source of his trials wasn't fully revealed until the end of the book, it really was the Lord who had brought them on him. And it wasn't without reasons. Good reasons. Necessary reasons.

At another time and place, another person, Joseph, told his brothers that they had meant his torment for evil but God had meant it for good (Gen. 50:20).

So it was with the apostle Paul. This was his testimony:

Lest I should be exalted above measure...a thorn in the flesh was given to me, a messenger of Satan to buffet me. (2 Cor. 12:7)

Now, it clearly was not Satan but God Himself who wanted to keep Paul from getting such a big head that his ministry would be destroyed. Of course, at the same time Satan was using the problem to buffet him, to make things difficult.

So it is with all of life. So it is with everyone. So it is with you. So it is with me.

Job Knew Better Than God

Job was called a *"blameless and upright"* man, one who feared God and hated evil (Job 1:1). Yet, when terrible trouble struck, he contended with God, reproved God, sought to annul God's judgment, and condemned God so that he might be considered righteous (Job 40:1–2, 8).

He didn't understand that he *"darken*[ed] *counsel by words without knowledge"* (Job 38:2). In his pain he was angry with God. He felt that God had no right to treat him this way. He could see no benefit from such treatment. None!

Job didn't see what he was doing. He didn't realize the awful extent of his proud and sinful heart. He wasn't ready to humble himself before God and His perfect, though inscrutable, will—not until God revealed Himself, took him to task, and showed him his folly, his inadequacy, his self-vindication, and his self-righteousness. Then Job abhorred himself and all that was not of God. Then he repented in dust and ashes. (See Job 42:6.) Then he freely, gladly admitted that he had spoken beyond his knowledge and had been too smart for his own good.

Seeing God As He Is Changed Job

At last Job saw God as He really is, not just as he had heard about Him. He could do no less than abhor all that was not of God and repent abjectly. (See Job 42:5–6.)

This is the story of everyone whom God loves and trusts enough to permit great suffering for eternal benefit.

But it isn't the end! Oh, no.

And the LORD restored Job's losses when he prayed for his friends. Indeed the LORD gave Job twice as much as he had before. (Job 42:10)

God met Job. Job met God. In meeting Him, Job was set free from himself, his arrogance, his conceit, his prideful independence, and his self-righteousness, so that he could gladly, freely pray for others. First came God Himself, then spiritual freedom, then prayerful concern for others, then temporal benefit.

As we see God and His dealings with us as they are, we, too, are set free from ourselves, our conceit, our prideful independence, and our self-righteousness. Then we can gladly allow God to do us good as He wills, in His own way—no matter whether the benefit He brings is in the temporal, physical dimension or in the eternal, spiritual dimension; no matter whether we see it now or not until eternity.

We need to remember that God does not always send us temporal benefits immediately following our pain. Sometimes we have to wait for eternity to receive the gain from the pain!

And it's just as well. Sometimes, upon their insistence, the Lord has given His people the desires of their hearts here and now but has sent leanness into their souls (Ps. 106:15). Then the benefit intended through their sufferings has been lost, and sometimes the pain has only increased.

What a horrible waste!

A Fantastic Story of Divine Love

One lady wrote,

> For months I've asked the Master Surgeon to get to the bottom of the things that have held me back from allowing the fullness of His presence in my life. I've cried, "I surrender, I surrender."

God allowed pain and fear to overwhelm her. But her letter tells us the end of the story:

> God sent me a message through a sister in the Lord. He cut through all the garbage and penetrated my heart. "My child, My love for you is not based on your doing. There is no sacrifice required to receive My love. It's a free-flowing river straight from the Father's heart to yours. Just receive it. Dive into the rivers of My love."

My perception of the Father had been distorted. I'd tried to have faith in my faith. But this only led to works and failure. I kept thinking, "When I get this area of my life together, then God will bless me." But now my sin had been exposed.

With this new revelation of God's love, I became so free from bondage. It was a miracle. I no longer lived in fear. I began to be able to trust God. Most importantly, I realized His unfailing love for me!

The tumor I had wasn't cancerous. The church raised over one thousand dollars for me. People showered me with every luxury. Thank you for being part of the miracle God has done in my heart.

Indeed, it was primarily a heart miracle! She met God and was freed from bondage to fear. She began to learn to really trust God.

Still Another Beautiful Story

Another dear lady told me that she didn't want to accept the truth that God uses everything for our benefit. Her husband left a constant clutter, especially on her dining room table! She didn't understand what good could come of that! I said she could accept even this as from the Lord for her benefit, or she could be constantly in an uproar with her husband. She chose to give it all to the Lord.

A few days later she phoned, saying, "Guess what. I came home and the mess was all gone!" I responded, "Praise God. You know, He doesn't always choose to answer like that!"

Months later she phoned. Quietly, almost casually, she told me she was having a cancerous breast removed. After the operation, she phoned again to tell me the Lord had given her incredible peace throughout the entire ordeal. He had prepared her heart in an insignificant matter to ready her to trust Him with something that shook her world.

Did God know what He was doing? He did! He always does. But He sometimes takes a little longer than we would like. My wife has had Parkinson's disease for more than a quarter century!

Back to the Beginning

Let's return for a moment to the first story of this chapter. When I first put it in print, I realized I could be in big trouble if the friend I spoke of saw it and was offended by my sharing her story while she was still suffering.

But, praise God, I did not need to fear!

When I finally reached her by phone, I read what I'd written of her story to her. There was a long pause at the other end. I asked, "No response?" She replied, "I expected more."

You see, she thought she'd told me the rest of the story, but she hadn't.

In the conversation that I described at the beginning of this chapter, I'd suggested that she was self-righteous. Afterward, she kept thinking about what I had said. Finally, God revealed her self-righteousness to her. She was instantly thankful that He had.

Peace and freedom replaced the awful strife and frustration. She saw that all suffering was working to perfect us. She was grateful that she had been counted worthy to endure suffering and to be made into God's image thereby.

She concluded, "As time goes on, the Lord's direction becomes increasingly clear; He continues to reveal how He wants me to respond to Him." And He isn't done yet!

If you can't come to the Lord as you would like, or if your coming isn't met with all the responses from God that you would like, just let Him work in His own time and way. Remember, the work isn't your doing but His. Let Him be God, fully in charge.

No, this approach isn't just another form of withdrawal or escapism. It's the best road to living in reality—God-centered spiritual reality. Though it may not seem so at first, little by little you'll be enabled to face the pain of your circumstances. You'll find the pain being replaced by confidence in God's ability to care for your eternal good, even through the very worst temporal circumstances.

Chapter 9

Why, Lord, Why?

Shall the one who contends with the Almighty correct Him? He who rebukes God, let him answer it.
—Job 40:2

The phone rang. The person at the other end was clearly distraught, so distraught I have to change the details of the story so that I don't cause unnecessary offense.

She was a Bible-reading, soul-winning Christian. But God hadn't met several of her needs for an unbelievably long period of time. They were needs that, according to her understanding of Scripture, God had promised to meet. And, instead of getting answers to her prayers, it seemed that her troubles just mounted up.

She didn't think she was angry with God. She hadn't lost her faith. But she was hopelessly frustrated. As much as she might have tried to avoid admitting it, the fact was she was thoroughly disillusioned.

Christianity that emphasizes doctrine alone has no answer for such a hurting heart. Nor does Christianity that emphasizes experience alone. Why? Because both expect God to change our circumstances to suit us, while God wants to use our circumstances to change us and draw us to Himself.

God's Great Desire for Us

God has one great wish for us. It is to draw us to Himself in love. And He permits every circumstance in our lives to come to us with that one purpose in mind. Every other reality of the Christian life must be viewed as secondary to this overriding truth. Failure to recognize and live by this fact is failure indeed.

The basic premise of the Christian life is this: *"Not* [my] *will, but Yours, be done"* (Luke 22:42). But the person whose concept of prayer is simply to ask and get from God will neither really accept this in his heart of hearts nor want to. Instead, he will end up constantly trying to manipulate God to get what he wants from Him.

It seems that God lets some people get away with this. Their success is the envy of other Christians all around. But, in reality, it may not be they who should be envied, but the poor hurting ones who face overwhelming difficulties. God may permit some to seem to succeed only because He knows they would never respond to great difficulties by seeking Him. On the other hand, His poor hurting children may be those whom He knows will, sooner or later, be driven to Him by their difficulties, and only by them.

Great Gain from Great Pain

Few, indeed, are those who don't need to face great difficulty, pain, or deprivation before they will respond wholeheartedly to God's love-call. In fact, it's doubtful whether there are any who will even hear His love-call with any clarity or urgency except through the pressure of pain.

*My son, do not despise the chastening of the
LORD, nor detest His correction; for whom the
LORD loves He corrects, just as a father the son
in whom he delights.*   *(Prov. 3:11–12)*

Real Pastoral Leadership

I got another phone call. It was from a dear pastor brother. He wanted me to know that my book *A
Christianity That Really Works* had impacted his life
and revolutionized his ministry. Now, he said, his
ministry had a power he'd never known before.

You can imagine how his words encouraged my
spirit—yes, and fed my ego, too. But my next response was, "Dear God, if he knew me as I know myself, he'd wonder how You could use me at all."

Then a deep concern for him stole into my heart.
"O Lord, let this change not be anything less than
casting this dear brother on You. May he not feel he's
finally got something he needs. May he know that it's
just You he needs, today and every day of the rest of
his life."

And my loving heart's desire for him now is that
he glory not in new power or new assurance or new
success, but in a new relationship with his God.

Paul's Example

Paul's thorn in the flesh was *"a messenger of
Satan to buffet* [him]" (2 Cor. 12:7), given to him by
God. Satan intended it for his harm. God intended
it for his eternal benefit. God gave it to him, and
God wouldn't take it away, not even in answer to
what Paul might have felt was the prayer of faith.

Its purpose was to keep Paul dependent on the Lord. And Paul valued that enough that he stopped asking to have it removed.

Who knows? Maybe God would have removed it had Paul kept asking. And who knows? Maybe Paul's usefulness to God may have dissipated, along with his intimacy with Him.

Instead, Paul said, "I'll go a step further. I'll glory not in my strength and ability, but in my infirmities. I'll take pleasure, not in my successes and capacities, but in my infirmities, reproaches, necessities, persecutions, and distresses. For it is when I am weak that I am strong." (See 2 Corinthians 12:9–10.)

No, Paul hadn't taken leave of his senses. He'd gotten them straightened out. He really was happy when reproached, in need, persecuted, and in distress.

And it is this my heart earnestly desires for my dear pastor brother. I want him to revel in the infirmities, distresses, and persecutions that drive him back again and again to his God, rather than in all the glorious experiences and wonderful successes he may ever know.

How about you? Are you willing yet to tell God it's okay to start straightening you out? Or are you still too afraid of the pain this may entail?

If you're already enduring infirmities, reproaches, necessities, persecutions, or distresses, are you willing yet to tell God it's okay, just so He accomplishes His own love-purposes in you?

Are you willing to start spending some quiet time with Him, worshiping Him, and learning to accept joyfully whatever He sends you to draw you to Himself in love and to make of you something of eternal usefulness to Him?

Chapter 10

Three R's and Then Some

The Almighty...shows no partiality to any
who are wise of heart.
—Job 37:23–24

Are you still a long way from living restfully, peacefully content with what God sends your way? Are you still angry, anxious, worried, frightened, frustrated, lonely, distressed, or depressed?

No matter how pleasant or how unpleasant your circumstances may be right now, it's likely that some or all of these words describe you to a T.

If you say that none of these words describe you, either you're not telling the truth, you're self-deceived, or God has been doing His work in you most wonderfully. If that last one is true for you, give Him praise!

Hope for All of Us

I just read in my book *A Christianity That Really Works* these words:

> We have no reason for tension to rule our lives. If we are weak enough, meek enough, willing enough to be needy, we can always,

upon recognizing the cause of our tension, relinquish it to Him.

The tranquillity of resting in Him can replace the tensions. Waves of rest will return after each resurgence of tension as we live in continuing preference for God and His order of peace, rather than for ourselves and our order of constant restlessness. This relinquishing and relaxing can lead to the beautiful release of rest, peace, joy, and liberty in the Lord that we may have only dreamed about.

Thank You, Lord!

Why Not More?

But why haven't we been experiencing more of this relinquishing and resting?

First, because of our three r's—our native rebellion, resistance, and resentment! That's right, they're native, or natural, to us. No matter how "nice," how "self-controlled," how "good" a person you think you are, you, too, will find that you always react negatively at first to any hurt or pain, regardless of how it's inflicted.

We all naturally tend to react in anger, no matter how differently our anger may be expressed. Then our peace is destroyed, our rest ended. And the tranquillity of those around us is often shattered as well. Our trust in God flees, and our agony returns.

Nonresistance

To see this reaction changed, we have to start living in a dimension that isn't native to our sinful nature. We must live in nonresistance, in release from our rebellion, resistance, resentment, yes, and our rage.

While I was writing this chapter, my wife needed me to help her to the bathroom four times in less than a half hour. This was after she'd wakened me several times during the night and I'd stayed up with her a couple of times and made her two breakfasts. And that's only a small part of the story!

If I hadn't been writing this particular chapter, I fear my response wouldn't have been so relaxed and kind. But I thanked God that He had allowed all of this to help teach me to live what I preach.

My natural reaction to everything I don't like has been anger. Only the grace of God ever makes it otherwise.

You face the same problem in however different a fashion. If you don't deal with anger forthrightly, you may face the most terribly hurtful consequences.

Non-Anger

Nonresistance is non-anger—or more correctly, dealing with anger by the wonderful grace and enabling of almighty God.

Nonresistance doesn't mean liking the unlikable, approving the unapprovable. It means accepting it for Jesus' sake, dying to ourselves for Jesus' sake (Rom. 6:11).

While nonresistance may be called non-anger, it really means relinquishing our anger, letting it go. It is saying to God, "It's okay. If nothing else, You're seeking to make of me a kinder, gentler, more caring, more gracious person. You're seeking to make me more Christlike, a better testimony to the grace of God. You're teaching me to rest contentedly in You.

"You can enable me to suffer gladly with You so that You may be praised. You can enable me to die to myself and my pleasure in order to live for You and Yours."

When we respond in rebellion, resistance, resentment, or even rage, our reaction may be perfectly "normal." But we're rejecting the peace that passes all understanding (Phil. 4:7), destroying our rest in the Lord, isolating ourselves from our God and the good He has for us, and doing immense damage to our bodies, minds, and emotions, as well as to our spirits and to our relationship with the God who is Spirit.

Stress to Blame

It's becoming increasingly common to lay at least partial blame on stress for almost every illness, including the two most common killers, cancer and heart disease.

Depression is becoming more and more common, and stress or tension is often blamed. Fortunately, a chemical imbalance is more and more frequently being seen as the major culprit, and there are many things a person can do to help correct this imbalance.

However, I want to emphasize the danger of harboring rebellion, resistance, and resentment and accent the need of almost instant nonresistance to whatever or whomever may be the immediate cause of our loss of peace and rest. There's no peace to be had except in this way.

Even if you feel that you are momentarily incapable of submitting to God, of letting go of your anger, at least you've been offered hope for the future, no matter how impossible your circumstances may be.

But why continue suffering so much more than necessary? And why cause so much unnecessary suffering to others? Why not accept the circumstances that God sends your way? Why resist them? Why continue in your anger—anger at the circumstances, anger at the people who cause the circumstances, and yes, believe it or not, anger at the God who permitted the circumstances?

Mad at God?

No, you don't have to believe that you get angry at God for allowing your difficult circumstances if you don't want to. I understand entirely. "How could anyone be angry with a perfect God?" we reason.

Well, even if God is perfect, we're not! And we do get disappointed with Him for not answering all our prayers. We do get frustrated with Him when we seek Him in prayer and He doesn't seem to be there. We do mistrust Him when He asks things of us that just seem to be too much. Those are all negative emotions we feel toward God. Anger is just one more, one a little less acceptable, one a little more difficult to admit.

The Merciful Stroke of Death

I'd like to continue quoting the passage from *A Christianity That Really Works* that I started to quote earlier in this chapter. It continues as follows:

We simply must die to having any hope in ourselves so it may all be in Him alone.

Only He can do what needs done.

"We had the sentence of death in our-selves, that we should not trust in ourselves but in God who raises the dead" (2 Cor. 1:9).

The passage goes on to say,

When the Christ-life demands our death, all that is of the old man rises up in rebel-lion....God offers us Himself and with Him every good thing. But the best, kindest, loveli-est, most wonderful gift He offers is our death stroke....He can live fully and freely only in those who have willingly accepted the slaying of their independent selves.

A part of accepting the slaying of our independent selves is accepting without resistance everything that comes our way as coming from God.

The only way to live in rest and peace is to live in nonresistance, accepting the least acceptable as coming from God's gracious hand of love.

Nonresistance! Really?

We find it extremely difficult at first to believe that God really does want us to accept all our circumstances without resistance—as coming to us from His good hand. After all, many of them are the result of sin. Some are sin in action. A lot of them will cause a good deal of harm. They may bring disgrace on the name of God and His Christ. So how, we ask, can we possibly accept all our circumstances without resistance? They may self-evidently demand resistance on the part of any responsible, godly person. To fail to resist them might be sin. Doesn't the Word say so?

Yes, it sure does! *"Resist the devil and he will flee from you"* (James 4:7). But isn't it ironic how we remember the second part of that verse and so conveniently forget the first? The first part reads: *"Therefore submit to God."*

These aren't the two separate thoughts we've made of them, but one thought with two halves. In order to properly resist the Devil, we must first submit ourselves to God. And this includes submitting ourselves to His permissive will expressed in the circumstances of our lives, no matter how unacceptable our humanity may find them.

This submission even includes the sins of others to which we're subjected. No, I didn't say we ought to approve of their sins! Never, never, never! But we ought to subject ourselves to God, who has allowed their sins to exist.

Why? How can this be? The omnipotent God, who has permitted their sins to exist, is seeking to bring from them praise and glory to Himself and eternal benefit to us.

God Is Still in Control

He hasn't lost control, even in a sinning world. He has simply permitted sin to exist for a time. Out of it all, He will ultimately be praised, and His people will benefit eternally.

Romans 8:28 is still in the Bible. It hasn't gone away!

> *And we know that all things work together for*
> *good to those who love God, to those who are*
> *the called according to His purpose.*
>
> *(Rom. 8:28)*

"All things" doesn't exclude anything. So, no matter how impossible it may seem, we need to accept God at His Word. Only after we've really submitted our hearts to the God who has permitted our circumstances—even those circumstances that we find least humanly acceptable—are we ready to properly resist the Devil and the sins and circumstances God allows him to produce or encourage.

Chapter 11

Help for the Unhappy

Give unto the LORD the glory due to His name;
worship the LORD in the beauty of holiness.
—Psalm 29:2

Oh come, let us worship and bow down; let us
kneel before the LORD our Maker.
—Psalm 95:6

How often do we feel hurt inside?
How often anxious?
How often frustrated?
How often alone, lonely?
How often frightened?
How often fearful?
How often discouraged?
How often discontented?

How often without God's rest and peace?
How often joyless, unhappy?
How often sinful?
How often guilty?
How often deeply ashamed?
How often angry toward others?

How often furious?
How often unforgiving?
How often unkind?
How often hateful?
How often selfish, self-centered?

How often unworthy of God?
How often unworthy of His love?
How often unworthy of His mercy and grace?
How often unworthy of our hope in Him?
How often unworthy of our place
and position in Him?
How often unworthy even of His salvation
from an eternal hell?

How often isolated from Him?
How often let down by Him?
How often disappointed in His failure
to answer our prayers?
How often out of fellowship with God?
How often out of harmony with Him?
How often more anxious to run away from Him
than to Him?

What Can We Do About It?

What can change the way we feel?
More importantly, what can change
the way we are?

Some suggest replacing negative thoughts
with positive thoughts.
Some say that deciding against the negative thoughts

will do the trick.
Some advise turning our thoughts Godward.
Some say just to trust God.
Some direct us to speak the word of faith.
Some demand we die to self and sin.
Some admonish us to consider our place in Christ
and His in us.
Some guide us to quote Scriptures.
Some want us to insist that God keep
specific promises He has made.
Some sing hymns, gospel songs, or choruses.
Others demand that we let go of whatever bothers us,
giving it all to the Lord.
Still others tell us to rebuke the Devil.

The Greatest Benefit

At one time or another, I've suggested many of
these ideas as ways you can benefit spiritually, ways
you can become a happy Christian.

Over the years, however, I've found the greatest
benefit from simply worshiping the Lord. If you worship the Lord best in song, sing to Him. If other practices help you more, go ahead!

I seem often to worship best and benefit most by
talking to the Lord about who He is in Himself and
who He is to me—or in just becoming nothing before
Him, silent and needy.

In my computer I've entered helps for my daily
devotions that I turn to many mornings. These con-
tain important Scriptures; my prayer list; some on-
going personal, intercessory, and ministry prayer
requests; and additional helps for worship.

Worship Any Time, Any Place

It's most important that we worship God in times set apart especially for seeking the Lord, and that we spend sufficient time with Him to really meet and fellowship with Him. If we don't, we may never learn to worship Him as we should.

But we can worship Him any time, any place. And we should learn to worship as we walk through the day with Him, just for the joy that our adoration brings to Him and to us. Our worship pleases Him and gives Him pleasure.

And we'll find ourselves happier, more content, if we pause in our hearts and spirits to worship Him frequently throughout the day.

Unhappiness, Trigger for Worship

Your very unhappiness may be a sufficient reminder to you to turn to the Lord in worship. And just a moment of worship is sometimes enough to banish the unhappiness, and sometimes, perhaps, even its cause.

We have a right to be at rest in the Lord regardless of our circumstances. But to strive in our own strength to turn our thoughts or feelings from the cause of our unhappiness to the Lord will often be futile and frustrating and will only add to our unhappiness. On the other hand, to go straight to Him in worship without thinking about our unhappiness or its cause will often be enough to put everything right.

Whether it's fear, anger, guilt, anxiety, unforgiveness, restlessness, or any other negative emotion or thought that troubles you and prevents your fellowship with God, it will often take flight in the presence of simple worship.

Simply Ignore Any Disinterest

Please, oh, please don't let the Evil One deceive you into thinking that you can't worship the Lord in the midst of your negative feelings. Don't let him convince you that to worship at such a time would be hypocritical.

Whether or not you feel like worshiping has nothing to do with it. The fact is that the Lord is always worthy of worship. The fact is that the redeemed, renewed spirit in you always longs to worship God. No matter how buried under the garbage of the day that longing may be, it's still there. It's still honest and true. And it is to these continuing realities that you may be responding when you worship Him in spite of every negative, hurtful feeling you have.

When we're immersed in negative emotions—feeling frustrated, hurt, angry, sorry for ourselves—we'll never feel like worshiping the Lord. When we worship no matter how we feel, we please God, we often benefit greatly, and we may even find our feelings changed. Try it!

Start learning today in your quiet time to worship God. Go on to turn your heart to Him in worship throughout the day. Let every unhappy, hurtful, negative feeling be a call to worship again and enter into His joy and rest. Be happy in Jesus! Be blessed!

Chapter 12

Worship Prayer Is Spiritual Dynamite

We are the circumcision [God's people], *who worship God in the Spirit, rejoice in Christ Jesus, and have no confidence in the flesh.*
—Philippians 3:3

If then you were raised with Christ, seek those things which are above, where Christ is, sitting at the right hand of God. Set your mind on things above, not on things on the earth. For you died, and your life is hidden with Christ in God.
—Colossians 3:1–3

The only hope there is of seeing a carnal Christian become a spiritual Christian, an unhappy Christian become a happy Christian, is for him to find his life in God. Our only hope, yours and mine, of seeing our failure and disappointment turned into hope is to find our life in God, in Christ. He alone is our hope.

This is one of the most freeing of biblical truths: *"Christ...is our life"* (Col. 3:4). May we never forget it.

But knowing this may be of no great value unless we discover some practical way of letting this glorious reality become freely operative in our lives. I believe God has revealed such a way to us, and I want all the world to know it.

Worship Prayer

The way is worship prayer. I've spoken of worship prayer many times in this book, although until this point I have not called it by that name. I introduced its practice to you a little more thoroughly in chapter 11. Now I want to help you make it the center of your life with God, beginning in your daily time alone with Him. Then in the chapters ahead, I'll try to guide you into ways to worship God that may well revolutionize your life, that may indeed help you return again and again to living happily, whatever life's circumstances may be.

Daily Devotional Prayer

What I'm suggesting in these chapters may be a new approach for you to your daily devotions.

Center your daily devotional prayer time on the Lord Himself. Whatever helps your attention to leave yourself and focus on your God, give that priority.

Talk to Him about your need of Him. Express any little bit of longing after Him that you may have. Tell Him you love Him, though you know that love to be so weak and poor. Thank Him for all His loving care for you. Praise Him that He loves you, that He cares for you, that everything He allows to happen to you is for your eternal benefit, that He never gives up on you, though you respond so poorly to His wooing. Or silently let your attention go lovingly to Him.

Special Helps

Read passages of Scripture that uplift the Lord, that encourage worship and praise and thanksgiving to Him. Read Revelation 1, 4, 5, 21, and 22, Job 38–42, worship psalms, Isaiah 6, Ezekiel 1, and so forth. Look up passages of Scripture in *Nave's Topical Bible* under "God," "Jesus Christ," "Holy Spirit," "Worship," "Praise," "Joy," "Peace," "Rest," "Hope." Listen to my *Psalms for Worship* tape. Sing hymns and songs of worship and praise.

Read one of the few books in print that uplift and magnify the magnificent person of God, that encourage worship and praise and thanksgiving. Among these are *Letters of Samuel Rutherford, Christian Book of Mystical Verse* by A. W. Tozer (out of print), *The Pursuit of God* by A. W. Tozer, *Rose from Briar* by Amy Carmichael, and *The God of All Comfort* by Hannah W. Smith.

Read especially chapters 13–16 and 26 of my book, *A Christianity That Really Works*. Pray chapter 14 and meditate on chapter 27 of this book. Read and meditate on "God Is Enough" at the beginning of this book and the Addendum at the end. Use both of these books as daily devotional guides. If none of these books help you, ask the Lord to help you find one that does.

Let God begin to become precious to you. Just let Him be God. Let Him move your attention from yourself to Him.

Talk to Him, not about you, but about Him. Wait quietly before Him if you can. Let Him speak love to your heart.

Return Often

Return to the quiet place as quickly and as often as you possibly can, either physically or in your spirit. Turn your heart to Him as much as you can, as often as you can. Whenever the Lord enables it, just let yourself go to Him without reservation. Agree with Him about your sin, discomfort, and dissatisfaction. But don't make much of it, lest it become a source of more worry and anxiety.

Come to Him as you're able, and keep coming. Don't come wanting anything from Him so much as wanting just Him. Let Him have more and more of your attention more and more of the time. Let the holy hunger you start to feel for Him begin to replace your self-concerns.

What Happens?

Now, when I worship the Lord in this manner, I frequently find that the tears begin to flow. My heart grows tender, my spirit sensitive, my will submissive, my mind responsive. I'm at peace and rest in the Lord. My worries and cares lose their importance in Him, His will, and His interests. All of this comes about in the most natural, spontaneous, effortless way.

I've sometimes felt quiet exhilaration, sometimes some degree of physical weakness.

The Lord often reminds me of some sin, failure, or need.

I may find myself praying petition or intercessory prayers that I don't think of as such. I'm simply discussing things with my loving heavenly Father.

Sometimes, reluctant to leave the place of intimate communion, I'll return to worship prayer and find the same responsiveness of heart all over again. This may occur many times in one devotional prayer time.

Sometimes it doesn't occur at all. When that happens, I tend to grieve as though I have lost a friend.

An Example

One recent prayer diary entry reads like this:

Tears, quietness, silence, stillness, meekness, humility, gentleness, absolute nonresistance.

Thank You for a God-receptive passivity of spirit. There's no adequate expression for it, nothing that cannot be misunderstood. Thank You that its heart is meek, humble, and gentle.

Thank You that this worship that goes beyond words, or even thoughts, continued off and on for some time, lessening and growing, departing and returning. This is YOU, present and speaking without words in the stillness. I give You praise, thanksgiving, and worship for Your presence. I recognize I'm so unworthy of it, but there's no self-condemnation in that recognition—just the rest, peace, and contentment that You give, and the recognition of Your acceptance.

Transmit this, I pray, into kindness and gentleness of spirit that continues throughout the day. Forgive me for being harsh with Ruthie this morning when she frustrated and exasperated me.

The Fruit

The result of this communion with this Friend is, little by little, the forming of the fruit of the Spirit in the life. In my own case, I wish the fruit were much greater. Yet I'm grateful that God can work some little bit of His life and character into this poor, needy, rebellious sinner by any means whatsoever.

The longer the time you spend alone worshiping the Lord with a submissive, responsive, sensitive spirit, the greater the spiritual transformation you may anticipate. Similarly, the more often you return to worship prayer throughout the day, the greater the rest, peace, joy, and liberty you may expect.

Get alone with the Lord as the psalmist did— three times a day (Ps. 55:17) or seven times a day (Ps. 119:164)—or every hour for a few minutes.

When you can't get physically alone, and whenever you're reminded of your need of the Lord, turn to Him in the chapel of your heart; worship Him as He enables. Let your spirit rest in His.

Your experience will undoubtedly be different from mine. Let it be. God knows your particular personality. Let Him tailor everything to you and your needs.

It took many months, frequent disappointment, and many hours alone with the Lord before any of this began to take shape in my experience.

Dangers

The first danger is that you may not spend enough time alone with Him. It took me endless hours to begin to see a spiritual transformation in my life. Regardless of the amount of time you need, no amount can be too much for the obtaining of the blessed results you will ultimately reap if you never give up, never quit.

That's the second danger: you may give up if there's a time when you don't get the results you're looking for. And there certainly will be.

I praise God that He didn't allow me to give up entirely through years of darkness and pain. Don't you give up either. Keep spending time with Him, seeking Him alone for Himself alone, no matter how futile your efforts may seem.

Your heart may not be prepared to forsake its carnal independence and self-dependence for the absolutely necessary neediness and poverty of spirit. Or you may be clinging to the resistance, resentment, and rebellion that I've spoken of. Or you may think you're worshiping while you're remaining as self-centered as ever.

If you've come to God for pleasurable feelings or for any other selfish reason, you may find the door to worship prayer barred. Your purpose in being there is not to please yourself, but to bring pleasure to the Lord Himself. Oh, wondrous thought!

The Open Door

Sometimes the open door to this worship prayer is honesty with God. Tell Him you're angry, frustrated, disappointed, jealous, envious, or whatever.

Let the telling be the admission of sin, wrong, and the need of God's transforming grace. But, as I say over and over, don't look for very long at yourself. There's little benefit there. Get your attention quickly back on the Lord.

Worship prayer is a return from ourselves to the God of love. There our self-consciousness is replaced by God-consciousness. Our natural drive to please ourselves is replaced by an instinctive inner desire to please and praise Him. Our spirits are being released to His Spirit so that His fruit is formed in us, and our whole world knows!

Without that tenderizing work of the Spirit in the time of worship prayer, I find myself remaining hard, angry, hurried, and self-centered. But with it, we are changed. The God we have so simply worshiped is glorified. We're finding our life in Him.

And, incidentally, we're building the basis for a genuine happiness such as we've never known before.

Chapter 13

The Greatest Thing in the World

*I also count all things loss for the excellence of
the knowledge of Christ Jesus my Lord, for whom I
have suffered the loss of all things, and count them
as rubbish, that I may gain Christ...that I may know
Him and the power of His resurrection, and the
fellowship of His sufferings, being conformed to
His death, if, by any means, I may attain to
the resurrection from the dead.*
—Philippians 3:8, 10–11

To walk with God in loving intimacy has to be
the most wonderful thing in the world. To
know Him. To love Him. To fellowship with
Him as friend with friend. To know that He cares for
every little thing about you and that He is entirely
capable of caring for every need you could ever have.
This has to be beyond compare the greatest thing in
the whole world.

While we may find great delight in enjoying this
greatest thing in all the world, it doesn't start with
us or with concern for ourselves. It starts with God's
concern for our interests and leads to our responsive
concern for God's interests. Nor can it long survive
on any selfish concern for ourselves. It survives only
on a God-generated concern for His eternal glory.

It is this God-centered focus that most Christians miss. They put their concerns first, whether for happiness or for the things of this world. Then they wonder why their relationship with God never grows into the loving intimacy that their redeemed spirits so instinctively long for.

When they pray, their prayers are about themselves and their desires. If they do pray for others, their prayers are very often out of a sense of obligation rather than love.

The Most Beautiful Lesson on Worship Prayer

One of Jesus' disciples asked Him to teach them to pray. And, oh, what He taught them! But it seems that most of us have missed what He so gloriously taught, missed it virtually altogether!

Let's look at it for a moment. We find these beautiful gems of truth in Matthew 6:9–13. I will be quoting from the King James Version.

"Our Father..." (v. 9). We're coming to the One who is our Father. We're leaving our self-centered selves and coming to the One who cares for us as a loving Father, One in whom we can place entire confidence.

"Which art in heaven..." (v. 9). Our attention is leaving the things of time and space, the temporal and physical, and going to what is eternal and spiritual.

"Hallowed be thy name" (v. 9). Our very first concern is that God be seen by all the world as the awesome God He is—to be venerated, honored, and worshiped by all.

"Thy kingdom come" (v. 10). We want God to reign supremely over us individually and personally

and over every other person and thing in His creation, and we want this to happen as soon and as fully as possible.

"Thy will be done in earth, as it is in heaven" (v. 10). We want what God wants to be done, in us and everywhere, as completely as possible. And we want the day in which it will be done absolutely to come as quickly as possible.

"For thine is the kingdom, and the power, and the glory, for ever" (v. 13). We worshipfully and gladly acknowledge that God alone is worthy to reign in power and glory for all the ages to come and to be praised for the perfection and eternity of His wisdom, power, and glory.

This is true worship prayer, and guess who taught it first? Our Lord taught it first, of course. And He taught it at the hungry-hearted request of his poor earthly disciples. You and I, following after them, can profitably pray this same prayer in the same spirit day after day for years to come.

But you say, "Hold it right there. You left out the prayers of petition."

Oh, you noticed, did you?

"I sure did," you say, "and this seriously distorts the Lord's teaching on prayer."

A New Look at His Teaching on
Petition Praying

Let's look at the missing petitions.

"Give us this day our daily bread" (v. 11). We look to our heavenly Father, Lord, and God for the supply of our real temporal needs as long as He leaves us here on earth. We look to Him alone, not to

our strong right arm, our job, our bank account, our accumulated wealth, our insurance, nor to government welfare or security programs. We look to none of these, but to God alone, so that He might be praised for supplying our needs, whether through ordinary means or through the most extraordinary means in the most impossible of circumstances. Yes, and the reason that we look to Him is indeed and alone that He might be praised.

George Müller ultimately fed two thousand orphans every day without telling anyone but God of his needs. One day they had no milk for breakfast. He told his heavenly Father about the need. Shortly, there was a knock at the door. A milk cart had broken down. The milk was going to go bad, and the driver wondered if they could use it!

According to Müller's own testimony, why did he start the orphanage? Not primarily to feed and clothe poor orphans. Not primarily to lead them to Christ. But primarily to prove to the whole Christian world that God could meet any need, no matter how large, in answer to trusting prayer only. God has been glorified ever since by the telling of this marvelous story around the world. If you haven't read it, you must.*

Yes, God has allowed some of His children to die as martyrs. That's His right and privilege. Through it, He has often been praised, and some of His children have been rushed the sooner into His glorious presence in peace. For every one of these instances, He has provided the daily physical needs of hundreds

---

* Müller's story can be read in *The Autobiography of George Müller* (New Kensington, PA: Whitaker House, 1984).

of thousands who have looked to Him, sometimes in the most impossible circumstances.

"Forgive us our debts, as we forgive our debtors" (Matt. 6:11). Surely this statement cannot be considered a demand. A demand on the part of the debtor against his creditor? Hardly. Rather it is a recognition of our deep neediness. It is a plea certainly, but a plea asked in the deepest humility and sense of unworthiness and need. Still, it is a plea asked also in the fullest confidence in the loving character of the Person of whom it is asked, and in His willingness and ability to forgive, cleanse, and make whole.

"Lead us not into temptation, but deliver us from evil" (v. 13). Keep us out of the path of temptation to which we would succumb, or else we surely would cave in. Now, why would we pray such a prayer? Because God has put it in our hearts to want not to displease Him, but to give Him pleasure. And this is what we're really asking—that we might please Him and give Him pleasure, now and forever.

Certainly I understand if you want to interpret this prayer otherwise. But I wonder if you're not, in doing so, depriving yourself of some of the wonders of worship prayer and of that moment-by-moment, intimate, loving fellowship and communion with almighty God that is the heart's desire of every redeemed child of God. I wonder if you're not depriving yourself of some of the joy of the greatest thing in all the world.

It's Neither Yours nor a Result of Your Efforts

In conclusion, let me remind you that the greatest thing in all the world is not something you can produce. It is God's. It is His alone.

Only those who are willing to be poor and needy will truly benefit from it. Only those who are brokenhearted over their sin. Only those who are willing to be humbled and made meek and lowly. Only those who are willing to be made like the lowly Christ of the stinking stable, the manger bed, the carpenter's shop, the despised city, the cursed cross, and the guarded tomb.

So the next time you come to God in worship prayer, come to Him alone for Himself alone. Come willing to be the needy person He reveals you to be.

If you come in self-dependence, self-confidence, or just plain self-centeredness, you're not really coming at all.

Let His revelation of your sin and need cast you wonderfully, hopelessly on Him who alone is your hope.

Let me conclude with the words with which I began this chapter: To walk with God in loving intimacy has to be the most wonderful thing in the world. To know Him. To love Him. To fellowship with Him as friend with friend. To know that He cares for every little thing about you and that He is entirely capable of caring for every need you could ever have. This has to be beyond compare the greatest thing in the whole world.

Chapter 14

Precious Prayer

O God, You are my God; early will I seek You; my
soul thirsts for You; my flesh longs for You in a dry
and thirsty land where there is no water.
—Psalm 63:1

Prayer for My Place in Christ

I accept my place in Christ—
accepted in the Beloved,
righteous and blameless in Him.
I thank You that He is in me,
empowering and enabling me
for all that pleases You
and brings You praise.
May I respond appropriately to You
in these great spiritual realities,
so that You will be
praised and pleased indeed.

Prayer for Victory over Spiritual Powers

I take my place
in the almighty Christ

under His shed blood
as the only safe place
for a sinner such as I.
From that position,
I join with You in opposition
to all the Evil One is doing
to destroy us and our ministry.
I trust You
to deny him access to us
in any way other than that which You
specifically design
for Your eternal glory
and the everlasting good
of us and others.
Be it so.

Worship Prayer

I worship, praise, love, adore, honor, glorify,
uplift, and exalt You.

You alone are worthy.
You are precious.
You are omnipotent, omniscient, omnipresent,
all-wise, eternal, infinite, unchanging,
perfect, holy, just, pure, lovely,
glorious, gracious, great, good, faithful, loving,
kind, merciful, and full of beauty.

You are the mighty God,
the everlasting Father,
Prince of Peace,
King of Kings,

Lord of Lords,
Alpha and Omega,
beginning and end,
creator and sustainer of all things.
You are my counselor,
guide, and guard,
bright and morning star,
dayspring from on high,
the Door, Way, Truth, and Life,
Light of the World,
Bread of Life,
spring of living water,
rock of my salvation,
anchor of my soul,
the citadel to which I flee,
lover of my soul,
delight of my spirit.

You are
the good and great Shepherd,
the altogether lovely One,
more to be desired
than gold and silver,
the lily of the valley,
the fairest of ten thousand
...no, fairer than all.

You are my love, my light,
my hope, my joy, my delight,
my salvation, my peace, my rest,
my supply, my sanctifier,
my wisdom, my righteousness,
my sanctification,

my redemption, my atonement, my help,
my enabler, my empowerer,
my strength, my shield,
my protector, delight of my life, my caretaker,
my Friend, my provider, my all in all.
You are the Great High Priest,
the living Word,
the great I AM,
full of grace and glory,
my refuge, my fortress, my God.
My dwelling place.

I love You.
I long for You.
I hunger for You.
I seek after You.
I desire You.
I hope in You.
Oh, that I might long for You more and more.

By Your gracious enabling
I wait quietly before You,
silent, meek, humble, nothing in myself,
in passive receptivity toward You alone.

I thank You that I am
complete in You,
that I live in You and You in me,
that You are my all in all.

Be uplifted, praised, honored, glorified, exalted,
magnified, worshiped, loved, and adored.

You alone are worthy of praise, adoration,
worship, glory, and honor.

Your angels worship
and praise You night and day.
So may we.

Draw me to You in love.
Enable me to focus
my attention on You,
center my affection on You,
meditate on You,
worship, praise, thank You,
seek You, long after You,
look to You,
hunger and thirst for You,
yearn after You, crave You,
make You my delight.

Help me to walk with You
in love, joy, peace, rest,
and quietness of spirit.

I thank You for all You are and do.

Petition Prayer

I desire that all I do
might bring praise to Your name.
Forgive me for all that does not, and change it,
I pray.

Be my teacher.
Instruct me. Correct me.
Cause me to obey You
and to make You first
in every practical way.

Thank You for Your Word
and for giving me
greater appreciation for it.
May it become increasingly precious to me.
Make it alive to me.
Instruct me from it.
Humble me to want to learn from it
as though I know nothing.

Prayer for the Church

Send revival
to Your church
throughout the world
in such a way that it will draw Your people
to Yourself in love,
that it will bring great praise to Your name
and result in multitudes of the lost coming to
know You as Savior and Lord.

Bless all Your ministers
and their ministries.
Draw them in humility,
meekness, and love to Yourself.
Teach them to rest in peace in You.
Then enable and empower them.
What I pray for myself,
I pray for them.

Prayer for Salvation

Bring my unsaved loved ones
and others

for whom I'm concerned
to repentance, faith,
and eternal salvation in Christ Jesus.

Final Prayer

In it all, humble me
and exalt Yourself
for the good of all.

Precious Lord Jesus, come again soon
and take us to be with You.

Chapter 15

When Worship Works and When It Doesn't

It is vain for you to rise up early, to sit up late,
to eat the bread of sorrows; for so
He gives His beloved sleep.
—Psalm 127:2

Wait on the LORD; be of good courage,
and He shall strengthen your heart;
wait, I say, on the LORD!
—Psalm 27:14

It's a wonderful thing to learn to worship the Lord. We'll be engaged in worshiping our wonderful, awesome God throughout an endless eternity. So we can't start practicing too soon!

Nor can we ever worship Him too often. In fact, it ought to be our aim to have our every thought colored with worship of our precious Lord and God. Even our very attitudes should be increasingly impregnated with the attitude of worship!

So it isn't too much to say that all our lives ought to be spent in learning to worship God. Still, this statement is only accurate when we realize that the emphasis isn't on our activity of worship, but on our object of worship—God Himself. Unless it is He who inspires the worship, unless it is He who enables the worship, unless it is He who empowers the worship, we can't really worship Him.

It Is He!

It is He we seek, nothing less, never anything less. To come to worship is nothing. To come to God by His enabling is beneficial beyond description for time and for eternity.

It is He we depend on, not ourselves. To depend on ourselves for anything, particularly for anything of a spiritual nature, isn't only a waste of time—it's spiritually harmful.

We can say worship words, but they become worship only when the Lord Himself enables, inspires, and empowers them. So, when we come to worship, we must come as we must always come to Him—poor, needy, humble, hopeless, and helpless without the transforming power of almighty God Himself.

Resting Contentedly at Home in Him

Our ultimate aspiration isn't to engage in active worship, but to abide in Christ, to be at home in God, peacefully, restfully, contentedly at home in Him, spontaneously loving Him, looking to Him, relying on Him, yielding to Him, heeding Him, learning about Him, serving Him, pleasing Him, worshiping Him, and so much more. He is the object and center of everything; we are insignificant except as we're attuned to Him and His eternal purposes. No, worse than insignificant, we are actually dangerous and damaging beyond our comprehension!

Recognize the albatross around your neck in the form of self-centeredness. Let the Lord begin to release you from your self-interests so that you can have your spirit centered on Him and His interests.

This may be difficult. Most of us have spent all our lives, even our prayer times, consumed by self-centeredness. We've known only one thing: asking for what we want—often, as James said, simply to consume it on our own lusts (James 4:3 KJV).

The focus of our lives should rather be to please God, to give Him pleasure. To the extent that this becomes our actual purpose, we will glorify God, bless others, and enjoy happiness and peace. To the extent that it doesn't, we'll live in loss, now and eternally.

Oh, how far we are from this ultimate aspiration! How near we are to being so terribly dangerous and damaging—so much nearer than we're often willing to give even momentary credence!

Living in Repentance

That's why we need to be living in constant repentance. Repentance for, or grief over, our sinful nature, as well as for our sinful actions, ought not to be an infrequent activity, but a constant attitude.

This isn't to say we should grovel in continual sorrow and pain. Hardly! That's all too likely to be more self-pity than genuine repentance. But we should be glad to have God reveal our sinful nature to us again and again. And we should be grateful when He reveals specific acts of sin that need to be repented of before Him and confessed to men whenever that's appropriate...and we'll find it appropriate far more frequently than we've ever dreamed.

Genuine worship of our perfectly holy God will almost always be accompanied by genuine repentance. An unwillingness to recognize and repudiate our sins will almost certainly close the door to genuine worship of this perfectly holy God.

Watching for Pretense and Hypocrisy

When worship prayer becomes the mere repetition of worship words, it's of little value. Worse, it may lead to self-satisfaction, pretense, and hypocrisy. When this happens, we're already in a relatively backslidden state.

Public praise is all too often practiced in this same hypocrisy and needs the same kind of repentance.

Worship prayer may become a farce if it doesn't lead ultimately to spiritual growth, increased love for God, increased responsiveness to Him and His voice and will. Please notice the word *increased*. Don't let the Devil discourage you by suggesting that you stop worshiping God in prayer because it's just empty repetition of words without real meaning. Instead, simply recognize the need of letting God search your heart to correct and instruct you and continue His transforming work.

Neglecting Worship Prayer

Even a few days without private times with God in worship prayer is enough to leave you feeling backslidden, guilty, and alone. So don't ever quit for any reason whatsoever.

When you've neglected worship prayer, when you seem not to be able to really worship Him even when you try, or when you feel separated from Him, let the Lord search your heart. Be prepared to just listen to His voice. Wait quietly on God. Be willing to be still before Him; no words are necessary, just a tender, responsive spirit. As He enables, rest in His peace.

Hoping in Him Alone

Remember that your hope is in Him alone. Don't return to striving and self-effort. But, as He searches your heart, let Him show you where you've become careless or disobedient.

See where you've allowed your desire for the things of this world to displace your desire for the Lord. Is time with the television, radio, newspaper, other reading, or idle chatter limiting your time with Him, His Word, and helps for your spiritual living? You'll find you can't seek God, you can't worship Him satisfactorily, while you're feeding the flesh (Rom. 8:8).

God, the living, loving Person, must increasingly become the focus of our interest and attention. Anything that distracts us from this process must be willingly sacrificed. This includes even, and perhaps especially, our sin. Repent, get it taken care of quickly, and get back to your primary business of worshiping God and rejoicing in Him.

If we would worship and rejoice freely in Him and know His rest and peace, His hope and freedom, we must increasingly accept in the depths of our spirits His absolute faithfulness, reliability, and trustworthiness. To do otherwise is to drive the wedge of unbelief and mistrust between us and Him. God forbid! Let us joy and rejoice in Him and His complete trustworthiness for us, and for all.

Recognizing Our Failures, His Victory

We would like to always live in victory by never failing our God, by always achieving His standards. But this kind of victory must wait for heaven. Between here and there, our victory is in constant, willing recognition of our failures; in our increasingly constant, willing repentance of our sin; in our recognition that only Christ in us is adequate to live His life in us in victory; in turning again, again, and again to Him in worship, submission, repentance, love, rejoicing, rest, peace, and utter, absolute dependence; in being willing, then, by His enabling, to deny ourselves, take up our cross, and follow Him (Matt. 16:24).

Never can living in rest in the Lord displace the necessity of willing obedience and glad self-denial. These are what living in wondrous rest in Him produces. Resting in Him leads us to know that the worst of sins is to pridefully think we're capable of obeying Him and denying ourselves without dependence on Him and the life of Christ in us.

Christ is all and in all. (Col. 3:11)

Christ in you, the hope of glory. (Col. 1:27)

Thanks be to God, who gives us the victory through our Lord Jesus Christ. (1 Cor. 15:57)

For of Him and through Him and to Him are all things, to whom be glory forever. Amen.
(Rom. 11:36)

Chapter 16

Too Capable

Have you an arm like God?...Then I will also confess
to you that your own right hand can save you.
—Job 40:9, 14

The next six chapters will show us some of the
bad habits that keep us from being happy regardless of our outward circumstances. How
can we be happy when we rely not on the infinitely
powerful God but on our ultimately incapable selves—
when we live in constant strife, serve not others but
ourselves, resist what God allows in our lives, hold
grudges, or live by our ever changing feelings?

Deceitful and Desperately Wicked

The heart is deceitful above all things, and
desperately wicked; who can know it?
(Jer. 17:9)

Believe it or not, this was one of my dad's favorite
Scripture verses! Shortly before he went home to be
with the Lord at eighty-three years of age, I told him
he was a better man than he'd ever been. Nonetheless,

we both knew he was living proof of the accuracy of this Scripture. For that matter, so am I!

The fact is that, without God's intervention, we're not going to be able to handle life well, whatever our circumstances may be. Jesus said, *"Without Me you can do nothing"* (John 15:5).

Though we wouldn't admit it, most of us still think our job as Christians is to achieve acceptance with God by our good behavior, our works. And we remain failures spiritually, living largely without the hope, love, joy, rest, peace, and liberty we've been promised. And, what's worse, many of us are going to stay that way.

Oh, how spontaneously the tears come to my eyes as I write this! We need not live this way.

The Top Is the Bottom

Many Christians tend to think that the height of spiritual achievement is living in a world of religious excitement—or that perhaps it's getting wonderful things from God, both religious and temporal. Along with this idea, many Christians have sometimes seemed to possess a pride of achievement, as though it were somehow they who were responsible for getting good things from God due to their proper performance. They think that they've pushed the right religious buttons and that they certainly deserve credit for it.

The idea that the highest pinnacle of the Christian life is a delightful, personal relationship built on resting contentedly and peacefully at home in the triune God is entirely foreign to many, and possibly quite unacceptable.

The top rung of the ladder of the spiritual life, and the bottom rung, too, is the kind of humility that, continually recognizing our failures, leads to a constant turning Godward that results in a continuous reviving of His life in us.

I said in *A Christianity That Really Works,*

As we constantly turn to Him in our need, He makes us weak enough and meek enough that to our weakness and meekness He can give Himself, His life, His rest, His peace, and all else we need.

Relish Your Inability

Ultimately, we must relish our inability, so that it might lead us to depend on His perfect ability alone.

Paul found spiritual success, not in the great crowds he addressed or the tens of thousands he led to Christ, nor in delightful answers to powerful prayers. He found spiritual success in God's refusal to grant a request that was undoubtedly at the top of his prayer list, and would have remained there all his life if he had refused to hear the voice of God saying, "No!"

Let me quote from Scripture this experience of Paul:

Lest I should be exalted above measure [get a permanent big head] *by the abundance of the revelations, a thorn in the flesh was given to me....Concerning this thing I pleaded with the Lord three times that it might depart from me.*

And He said to me, "[NO,] *My grace is sufficient for you, for My strength is made perfect in*
[your] *weakness."* [Paul responded:] *Therefore
most gladly I will rather boast in my infirmities,* [I'll be glad for them so] *that the power of
Christ may rest upon me....For when I am
weak* [in myself], *then I am strong* [in Christ].
(2 Cor. 12:7–10)

Only when we're willing to be weak, incapable,
nothing in ourselves, can we be needy enough to turn
to our God and let Him meet our needs and bring
about the wonderful things of which He alone is capable.

No Sad Story Here

A dear friend and supporter wrote,

My story may sound sad, but it's not.
That's because of you and Ruthie, and your
letters, tracts, and book! Through these, my
faith in Christ has grown, so that when my life
began to go down, down, I held onto my faith
in God.

Here's the story: My income went from
$420 a week to $400 a month. One of my
daughters had a breakdown. My son-in-law
had to file chapter 7 bankruptcy. My youngest
daughter went to jail for getting overpayment
of unemployment benefits. My sister's daughter wouldn't let any of the family see her children.

Oh, Brother Marr, God said, "Let Me handle it." Then, one night, He woke me at about

2 A.M. and laid my daughter on my heart. As I was praying for her, her sister-in-law called to tell me what was happening to her. And you know, I believe that if God hadn't led me to pray for her, someone would have shot her. Now, praise God, she's back home with her husband and children, looking for a job so she can help him.

My youngest daughter is working and paying the money back.

I've paid all my bills this month except one not due yet. God didn't send the money in hundred dollar bills. Oh, no, it came five dollars here, ten dollars there.

What a wonderful God we serve. He does His best work when we're stuck in the quicksand and can't move! Yes, be still and know that He is God (Ps. 46:10).

Thanks, Brother Marr, for letting me see God's work in your life. Through you I learned that not every day for a Christian will be an Indian summer; there'll be storms, too. I'm praying for you.

I praise God we were able to help prepare her for the storms that threatened to sink her ship. I praise Him that when she got into the quicksand she could look to the God who does His best work when we're hopelessly stuck. I praise Him that she had learned to listen to His voice so she could hear Him saying, "Let Me handle it." And again she could hear His voice in the middle of the night calling her to pray for her daughter who was in mortal danger. I praise Him for being there for her in her hopelessness and need, as He is for all of us when we're needy and have no hope except in Him and in the hope and help He alone can give.

It's when we're able to tackle the task before us, it's when we're capable of caring for our own needs— or think we are—that we're in trouble.

Are you unhappy in the midst of the troubles of life? You can be happy in Him, if you recognize your own incapability and His absolute capability. Let go of the struggle. Do the humanly foolish thing. Turn in simple neediness to Him. Worship, praise, and thank Him. Rejoice in Him. Watch the load lift.

Christ is all and in all. (Col. 3:11)

Whatever you do in word or deed, do all in the name of the Lord Jesus, giving thanks to God the Father through Him. (Col. 3:17)

Chapter 17

Quarrelsomeness

And a servant of the Lord must not quarrel but be gentle to all, able to teach, patient, in humility correcting those who are in opposition, if God perhaps will grant them repentance, so that they may know the truth, and that they may come to their senses and escape the snare of the devil, having been taken captive by him to do his will.
—2 Timothy 2:24–26

Quarrelsomeness is something else that may keep us from being happy regardless of our circumstances. And unhappiness might bring with it some dreadful results. It might make victims of us, not only spiritually, but emotionally and physically, too.

I published the *Christian Inquirer* newspaper for many years. Much of that time, I quoted 2 Timothy 2:24 in every issue: *"The servant of the Lord must not strive"* (KJV). Yet both the paper and my daily life gave evidence of the very strife, or quarrelsomeness, that Paul denied us the right to.

Full of Strife

Churches are full of strife. The third and fourth chapters of the book of James describe all too many churches all too well.

117

It is easy to point the finger at others. But if our hearts are honest, they'll deprive us of such luxury, and we'll point the finger right back at ourselves. We've been the culprits.

How Do I Know?

I can make that statement because I know my own heart. Furthermore, I know that the strife that naturally resides there lives just as naturally in every human heart. I know, too, from sad personal experience, that all the strife doesn't dissolve and disappear from the human heart as soon as the individual is born again of the Spirit of God.

No matter what spiritual experience a Christian may profess, his pride, arrogance, conceit, vanity, envy, jealousy, and self-will manage to show their ugly faces as strife or quarrelsomeness again and again.

How I thank the Lord, though, that I know something else from blessed personal experience, incomplete and imperfect as my experience is. What I have learned is this: to the extent to which we worship and praise our God and live contentedly at home in Him, God can replace the strife in the human heart with a surpassing gentleness of spirit.

Yes, He can, and He will. He will to the extent to which we give Him the opportunity. He won't force His gentle spirit on us any more than He will force on us His eternal salvation or any other of His good gifts. He waits for us to respond to His constant wooing.

Turn from Self and Strife

When we turn from ourselves and our inner striving to God and His inner peace, He can give us His rest, His joy, His liberty, and His incredible gentleness of spirit.

But we may try and try to obtain these things and never find them. Why? Just because we do try, instead of actually turning from ourselves and our self-efforts to Him.

It Takes Time

To begin learning to actually turn from ourselves to Him may take us hundreds of hours alone with Him. There we seek Him for Himself alone. And there we learn to see Him as entirely trustworthy, so that we never need to struggle and strive as though we had no God to take care of things for us.

That the process may take so long isn't strange. After all, we've spent a lifetime thinking of ourselves, centering everything on ourselves. That's simply a bad habit, the root of all other bad habits.

Then, having given the Lord the necessary time daily to get our attention on Him, we face another disappointment. Entering into His peace in the quiet time isn't enough. We still end up living much of the day in the same kind of heart strife that generates pain and distress inwardly—and the strife with those around us that generates still more pain and distress.

Inner strife is often more to blame for our distress, disappointment, and depression than outward circumstances. It can deprive us of the ability to be happy regardless of our circumstances.

119

Not Once but Always

As I've said so often, we must learn to turn in worship to Him and His peace again and again throughout the day. On each new reminder, on each new provocation, withdraw from yourself and other people and turn to the Lord in your heart or spirit, and there enter into His peace, no matter what the external circumstances may be.

Little by little, may you find the habit growing, the peace abiding, the gentleness of spirit increasing, and the strife subsiding.

Just think, my dear friend, of how many people might suddenly take an interest in the Christianity that really works as they see God's love, joy, and peace transforming you into a remarkably different kind of person.

Is It a Worthwhile Quest?

Will you begin today?

You'll notice I didn't ask, "Will you preach it?"

No, the question is, "Will you begin today to turn more and more to the Lord, letting Him teach you increasingly to live in Him, His peace, and His gentleness of spirit?"

Chapter 18

The Servant Heart

*Let nothing be done through selfish ambition or
conceit, but in lowliness of mind let each esteem
others better than himself....Let this mind be in you
which was also in Christ Jesus, who, being in the
form of God, did not consider it robbery to be equal
with God, but made Himself of no reputation, taking
the form of a bondservant, and coming in the likeness
of men. And being found in appearance as a man, He
humbled Himself and became obedient to the point of
death, even the death of the cross. Therefore God also
has highly exalted Him and given Him the name
which is above every name, that at the name
of Jesus every knee should bow.*
—Philippians 2:3, 5–10

For a long time I used to sign my letters, "Your
servant for Jesus' sake," using the terminology
of the apostle Paul in 2 Corinthians 4:5 (KJV). I
was serving the church extensively, providing much-
needed information and perspective. In that sense, I
certainly was their servant. And that was how I
wanted to be seen. However, in my heart and attitude, I don't think I was really a servant, or, more
specifically, what I call a servant/slave.

A Slave to Others

I have a little better idea now of what it means to be a slave to another human being, though my fleshly nature does not like it a bit better!

My wife may require my care any hour of the day or night. Her needs must come before my interests, regardless of what those interests might be. This means getting up several times each night, sometimes staying up an hour or more with her. It means sometimes massaging her, sometimes sitting in the chair while she does her best to calm her body and mind by trying with great difficulty to play the organ. And the situation is better now than it used to be! Before, there were times when I combed her hair literally by the hour to relieve the tension she endured.

Then there was the night when in a motel near beautiful Banff I thought we both would be driven crazy. Hour after hour, nothing I said or did brought any relief from the terrible, indescribable tension her body and mind were experiencing.

Meeting her needs still means letting her interrupt my sleep, my prayer time, my ministry time, my work time, sometimes every few minutes. It has meant getting to the store only to turn around and go home without getting in the door.

Frankly, being a servant hasn't been a whole lot of fun. And sometimes, I confess, I've objected loudly. Sometimes I haven't sounded a whole lot like a servant/slave. Sometimes I've sounded much more like a belligerent master. Lord, forgive me.

Servanthood Is Our Right Role

But the role of a servant is the one the Lord has called us to. It is the only role that will make us winsome Christians—believers who, by all means, "win some" to Christ (1 Cor. 9:22).

More than this, it's the only role in which a Christian can be happy. When we're out of harmony with the Lord, we're unhappy. And we're out of harmony with Him when we're not servants in heart and attitude. He came to serve and to die. Can we do less?

In our old nature, we're incredibly self-centered. We're incredibly proud. We're incredibly hateful. We're incredibly unkind. And if you don't think that's your old nature, you need to get alone with God and let Him expose you to yourself. Only He can make you willing to see yourself as you really are, though your old nature should be perfectly obvious. When you're imposed upon, stolen from, spoken unkindly to, put down, neglected, maligned, misrepresented, or hurt, how do you respond? Of course, you always react kindly, gently, meekly, graciously, lovingly, and thoughtfully. Don't you? You follow the example of the Hebrews, do you not?

You had compassion on me in my chains, and joyfully accepted the plundering of your goods, knowing that you have a better and an enduring possession for yourselves in heaven.
(Heb. 10:34)

Sure we do!
Look out! The sparks will fly!

123

We don't want to "take it." We want to "let them have it."

And, if outwardly we don't explode, inwardly we seethe. Our anger boils in what we think is silence. And that "silent" anger brings potent suffering to our bodies, to our minds, and to those around us. Far from being happy and healthy, we're sullen, peevish, fretful, depressed, sickly, and worse—even in fairly normal circumstances.

Our Place Is to Serve Others

It's the place of Christian servants to please others, not ourselves. It's our place to die to our own wishes and to live for the wishes of God and others. It's our place to give and give and give some more— to give sacrificially, not to take.

> *We then who are strong ought to bear with the scruples of the weak, and not to please ourselves. Let each of us please his neighbor for his good, leading to edification. For even Christ did not please Himself; but as it is written, "The reproaches of those who reproached You fell on Me."* (Rom. 15:1–3)

What a marvelous example Christ gave us! When He was maligned, He did not answer back. (See Isaiah 53:7.)

Can We Be Bosses and Servants, Too?

There is one situation in which our willingness to be a servant/slave is severely tested—the situation in which we are, in fact, in charge. In the places in which we are bosses, to be anything less is to disappoint those who are under us. Positions of authority include president of a company, supervisor, classroom teacher, policeman, courtroom judge, parent, to name just a few.

How can one be both boss and servant/slave at the same time? To fulfill both roles is possible only when we are servant/slaves in heart and attitude. Our heart, our attitude, is that it's our privilege to serve those whom we must also supervise.

This attitude shows in the tone of voice with which we instruct or correct. It shows as we manifest patience where impatience would be our natural response—even seemingly the appropriate response. It shows as we exercise mercy in place of mere justice. It shows as we're kind, concerned, or loving, even when judgment or discipline must, for the sake of the recipient, be severe. It shows when anger, rage, hatred, or violence displayed against us, even by those from whom it is least permissible, is met by a kind response. Only the grace of God can make that reaction possible, as I'm sure you know!

The Household Test

There is a test that this kind of servant/slave heart and attitude rarely survives. It occurs in your own home. When your expectations of being loved, accepted, respected, and even appreciated, are not met, how will you react?

If you're the Christian head of the home, you are likely to fail miserably—even if you've done well in the outside world. You are even more likely to fail if the imposition seems to you to be foolish and unnecessary.

I will give you an example from my own life. During the night, Ruthie locked a door that needed to be unlocked. When, from my bed, I asked her why, she said, "I can't think!" After decades of taking large doses of a potent hallucinatory prescription drug, it's a wonder she can think at all! But understanding and sympathy are sometimes sparse when mixed-up thinking pulls me out of bed, seemingly unnecessarily, for the fourth or fifth time in one night. However, it is in situations like this when a servant/slave attitude is needed.

Human Understanding Not Enough

Human sympathy and understanding, like a mere desire to have a servant heart and display a servant attitude, are of minimal value. They will most often let us down when they're put to the test. Our old nature will always come down on the wrong side. It will always do us in. Only the Christ-life will succeed.

How do we display the Christ-life? Wrong question! How does the Christ-life grow and expand within us until it cannot help but display itself? That's the question.

The answer will sound familiar, but it's the only one I have: Our hearts and spirits turn Godward. We worship. We praise Him. We rejoice in Him. We cast ourselves on Him. We find peace and rest in Him.

We come to Him in our need as often as we can—in prayer times, times of temptation and special trouble, and simply any time throughout the day. We respond to His love-call within by lifting our hearts and spirits to Him in worship, adoration, praise, thanksgiving, and love as often as we can.

We worship Him with words or in silence. It does not matter which, as long as our worshipful attention is drawn to Him.

Come in Humble Need

When we come in need to Him, we do not come to have self-interests met. On the contrary, we come because we recognize that we are unable to live the Christ-life apart from the dynamic operation of Christ Himself and His Spirit within. We recognize that only He is capable of meeting our needs with the dynamic of His life.

When you come, come trusting Him to remove your foolish pride and independence and replace it with a gentle, kind, meek, loving humility and dependence on Him. When you come, come seeking to find Him in His rest and peace. Come recognizing that everything He permits in your life—every pain, test, and temptation—He permits so that out of it He might bring eternal good to you and others, and glory to Himself. Ask Him to enable you to receive difficult circumstances gladly so that your good and His glory may be more fully promoted. This is the servant heart and attitude to which you aspire.

Note carefully: no contrary attitude will allow you to be happy in spite of what is happening in and around you.

Allow me to end this chapter in the way that I used to end my letters:

Your servant for Jesus' sake.

Chapter 19

Forgiving the Unforgivable

*Therefore if you bring your gift to the altar, and there
remember that your brother has something against
you, leave your gift there before the altar, and go your
way. First be reconciled to your brother, and then
come and offer your gift. Agree with your adversary
quickly, while you are on the way with him, lest your
adversary deliver you to the judge, the judge hand
you over to the officer, and you be thrown into
prison....Love your enemies, bless those who curse
you, do good to those who hate you, and pray for those
who spitefully use you and persecute you, that you
may be sons of your Father in heaven; for He makes
His sun rise on the evil and on the good, and sends
rain on the just and on the unjust. For if you love
those who love you, what reward have you? Do not
even the tax collectors do the same?*
—Matthew 5:23–25, 44–46

C hristians who hold a grudge against anyone
are, among other things, unhappy Christians
and hurting Christians. They put unnecessary
pain and stress on themselves, adding to the tensions
that life's circumstances are already piling on.

A lady who was working for me told me how, when she let go of the bitterness that had characterized her life, her arthritis got substantially better. Her unforgiveness had been literally poisoning her.

Another dear Christian lady wrote,

> I wish God would inspire you to write a message on forgiveness. I really have trouble forgiving people when they hurt me. I've prayed about and struggled with this for years.

She continued,

> I heard a preacher say that...if someone hurts you but doesn't ask you to forgive him, you don't have to forgive him. He asked, How can you forgive if he doesn't ask forgiveness?
>
> I'm afraid I don't agree....I know that according to God's Word we have to forgive in order to be forgiven. Pastor Marr, pray that I'll overcome this unforgiving spirit.

Unforgiveness Isn't the Problem

Are you surprised when I say that unforgiveness isn't the problem? Well, it's true, dear one. Your unforgiveness isn't the basic problem—it's you! Now, I know that's not the answer you wanted to hear. But it's the only answer I have for you.

We have a basic problem, all of us. It's ourselves. We love ourselves. We don't love that other person. Nor can we honestly say with much assurance that we really love God. Our love for Him is shallow and superficial at best. Because we love ourselves, we're easily hurt. We're readily angry. We tend to get bitter and even hateful. There are times when deep inside we would prefer to destroy rather than build, to hurt rather than help.

You're a Good Person

Now, perhaps you think I've gone too far! You think that this description doesn't fit you at all. You feel that you're really a very good person who just happens to have a little difficulty forgiving people who hurt you. After all, you say, who doesn't?

So you go right on being unable to forgive others—and really not being quite able to forgive yourself for not being able to forgive them.

Now, face it, dear one. As long as you think you're basically a good person who just happens to be the victim of imperfect heritage and surroundings, you're going to have trouble forgiving others. You're going to expect them to behave as you think you would—to be as good as you think you are!

The following expressions are dead giveaways of this kind of attitude:

"I wouldn't do that."

"I wouldn't act like that."

"I wouldn't behave that way."

These kind of statements show your self-righteousness.

"Self-righteous!" you explode. "Not me."

Listen, my dear friend, we have no clue as to what awful sinners we really are, how undeserving we are of God's forgiveness—or of anyone else's. And until we learn this, we'll never do well at forgiving others. So ask God to begin showing you your terrible, hopeless depravity and sin.

Now, as the sinners we are, we can't forgive! And, worse than that, we can't change, and we can't readily learn to forgive.

But there's Someone who can do it all.

Let's Face Reality

But before we talk about Him, I want to talk about our need to face ourselves realistically, to stop playing our self-righteous games of pretense. We need to face the fact that our sin of unforgiveness may be more serious than the offender's offense.

What if God wouldn't forgive you because you didn't deserve it? You would never get His forgiveness, would you? Yet we often won't forgive others because they don't deserve it. With this attitude, what awful harm are we doing to others, and to ourselves?

We can't stand the fact that the other person won't admit he's wrong, though we're just as unwilling to admit that we're wrong. After all, why won't we forgive? Because our pride has been hurt— our dignity, our self-esteem, our good name, our vanity. We're just not going to forgive him until he knows how he's wronged us! No way!

If that attitude continues, we're never going to learn to forgive the way God wants us to forgive. He wants us to forgive just the same, whether the offender will recognize that he's offended us or not.

Some people have never learned to be wrong, and some never will. They just can't admit they're wrong. So, if you wait for them to admit they're wrong, you'll wait a lifetime and still never hear an admission of guilt. Don't let them keep you down at their level. Remember that your offense of unforgiveness, even toward those who seek no forgiveness, may be greater than their offense against you. That's right—*greater!*

God's Forgiveness Is Free

Now, you may question why we should forgive those who are unrepentant if God doesn't.

First, God loves the sinner. He's married to the backslider (Jer. 3:14). He has no problem with loving the unlovely because He is love (1 John 4:8). That's why He loves you and me. We, on the other hand, have difficulty loving others. When we say we can't forgive them, what we're really saying is that we can't love them.

Second, God's forgiveness is part and parcel of His redemption, cleansing, and reception of the child who has been newly born into His family—and the beginning of His transformation of him. The only way He could provide these wondrous gifts to the unrepentant would be to force these gifts upon them against their will. And this, because of His own prior commitment, He neither will nor can do.

Forgiving the Most Unforgivable

Now, there's something more to face realistically. You must forgive even the most unforgivable. If you can't forgive the most unforgivable, you can't really forgive anyone! In every individual case, you need to see how really unforgivable the offender is. Don't pretend he's better than he is. See him as the sinner he is, just as you see yourself as the sinner you are. See him as the foolish, unkind, thoughtless, prideful, or selfish person he really is.

Otherwise, you'll remain enmeshed in those silly games of pretense, living where the God of truth and reality does not live. And you'll try to forgive a little where only a lot of forgiveness will do. You do not need to forgive a make-believe nice person who has been victimized by his circumstances; you need to forgive that nasty person who simply doesn't deserve forgiveness. And for this, only God is adequate!

Yes, we need to see ourselves as we are. We need to see the person who has offended us as he really is. But then, we need to look away from ourselves and the offender to the Lord, who alone has what it takes to love and forgive the unlovely and the unforgivable.

It's Not Our Forgiveness but His Life

Read this Scripture carefully. You'll find capsulized in it much of what I've been saying about forgiveness.

> *Christ is all and in all. Therefore, as the elect of God, holy and beloved, put on tender mercies, kindness, humility, meekness, longsuffering; bearing with one another, and forgiving one another, if anyone has a complaint against another; even as Christ forgave you, so you also must do. But above all these things put on love, which is the bond of perfection. And let the*

> *peace of God rule in your hearts, to which also
> you were called in one body; and be thankful.*
> *(Col. 3:11–15)*

We will not really be able to forgive as long as we live as our independent selves or look to our independent selves. But we are in Him, as He is in us, once we are His children by faith. We can rest in peace, at home in Him, relying on His life and power working in us to do what we can never do.

Let Go! Die!

Living in this reality, in union with Him, we can learn to let go, to relinquish everything to the Lord: our rights, our anger, our bitterness, our hatred, our lovelessness, our frustration, our self-righteousness—yes, our very lives.

Just commit everything to Him. Let go of your negative reaction in each new circumstance—whether it's unforgiveness, anger, fear, anxiety, or whatever it may be.

We must die to ourselves and all our rights (Rom. 8:13), as well as to our dignity, our good name, our popularity, our prestige, our property—yes, even to our awful self-righteousness.

We Can't. He Can.

To try to love the offender is futile. We can't. But, praise God, the One who is in us can.

To try to forgive the offender is to live in frustration. We can't forgive. We must allow the Lord to change us from the inside out until we're able, by His enabling, to gladly and freely turn the offender over to the One who does love him so that He can work the very best he'll allow Him to do for him.

When He enables us to forgive, it's only with the love with which He first loved us and forgave us when we deserved neither love nor forgiveness (Rom. 5:8). When He enables us to forgive, it's only by the mighty life of Christ within, and His all-encompassing love.

> *Looking unto Jesus, the author and finisher of our faith....Looking carefully lest anyone fall short of the grace of God; lest any root of bitterness springing up cause trouble, and by this many become defiled.* (Heb. 12:2, 15)

The extent of our capacity to forgive will be directly proportional to the freedom we give the Lord to live His life in us. My dear friend, no matter what the question is, the answer to the Christian's concerns is in Christ Himself. He is our life (Col. 3:4). We have no other. To look elsewhere is to remain frustrated. He is our hope. There is no other. It is His life living in our lives that alone makes anything different, that makes all things possible (Matt. 19:26).

Really now, isn't discovering this truth better—a million times better—than simply learning a superficial technique of how to forgive?

Chapter 20

Living in Sweet Harmony

*Therefore if there is any consolation in Christ,
if any comfort of love, if any fellowship of the Spirit,
if any affection and mercy, fulfill my joy by being
like-minded, having the same love, being
of one accord, of one mind.*
—Philippians 2:1–2

L iving in sweet harmony! What a beautiful ideal—to live our lives in sweet harmony with God and man. Still, as beautiful and desirable as it may be, it's not the easiest to achieve.

We're All Unique

A place to start may be with the realization that the relationship of every Christian with his God is uniquely and blessedly different. The God who makes every snowflake after its own pattern makes every human being different. He's able to respond to each person's uniqueness in ways designed to best meet his needs, provide the finest fellowship with Him, and make best use of the potential He gave him to serve Him and others.

What God asks of one He does not necessarily ask of another. What constitutes a realizable degree of sweet harmony for one is not the same for another. Some of us have a lot further to go than others....Just ask *me!* Some of us find our circumstances more difficult and demanding than others....Just ask *me!*

For this reason, we must be careful not to judge our brothers and sisters in the Lord superficially.

Sacrificial Service a Key

Instead, we can learn to say with Paul from our hearts, *"We do all things, beloved, for your edification"* (2 Cor. 12:19). We are privileged to serve man as well as God. And there's no harmony without glad, sacrificial service.

Out of our heart-service grow blessings beyond measure, not only for others, but also for ourselves. Among these blessings is the sweet harmony for which our spirits long.

Admit Your Native Selfishness

To sacrifice our own leisure and pleasure for God and others may have been natural to mankind before the Fall, but no more. Now, unfortunately, we are natively selfish, self-centered, me-oriented people.

Only God the Spirit can change this fact. And He can change it only as we agree with Him and willingly acknowledge our selfish spirit. We need to constantly recognize and confess our sinful selfishness, both in general and when it shows itself in specific instances.

When our egotism leads us to do or say things that ignore, belittle, irritate, carelessly impose upon, or otherwise hurt others, we need to willingly, open-heartedly admit our actions as the sins they are to the person we hurt.

This is a good place to further the process of learning to bend to God, His Word, and His will.

It's a good place to further the process of learning to live in sweet harmony with God—Father, Son, and Spirit.

It's a good place to further the process of learning to live in sweet harmony with others of our sinning race.

I've deliberately chosen to use the unusual expression *further the process of learning*. A learning process should be going on every single day of our lives. And, if we're born-again children of God by faith, we aren't just beginning the process now; we're taking a new step of increased commitment to that process and the God of that process.

Our Delightful God Does It

What a delight to be learning to live in joyous harmony with God and man! The fact that this harmony exists is not because of perfection on our part or that of others, but because of the perfection of our God. He perfectly understands our inadequacies, our incompetence, our failures, our sins, and our sense of guilt. Not only does He know and understand them, but He accepts us in spite of them. He accepts us in His Son through the sacrifice of His blood—His finished work on our behalf.

139

God loves us just as though we were as perfect as He is. Because of His perfections, God can do this without lessening His recognition of our shortcomings, without reducing His efforts to make us more like Him.

Our harmony with God and man exists and grows because Christ lives within us with dynamic life, working always to do us good.

Die in order to Live and Love in Harmony

This harmony thrives as we learn to die to our own desires and live in increasingly sacrificial love, caring, and giving. This sacrificial love is the opposite of the egocentric selfishness that destroys our relationship with God and man.

Paul learned to maintain this harmony in spite of his weaknesses and those of his children in the Lord. (See 2 Corinthians 12.)

An Absolute Trust

Paul went so far as to trust God implicitly with all the nastiness of life. Incredibly, he was honestly able to say,

I take pleasure in infirmities, in reproaches, in needs, in persecutions, in distresses, for Christ's sake. For when I am weak, then I am strong.   *(2 Cor. 12:10)*

This leaves no room for anger, hatred, and bearing grudges against the people—even, perchance, brothers and sisters in Christ—whom we see as the perpetrators of our persecution, the designers of our distress.

God had told Paul that he needed a thorn in the flesh to keep him from being puffed up with pride. (See 2 Corinthians 12:7-9.) Instead of rebelling and losing his harmony with God and man, Paul said, in effect, "If You can use that difficulty to keep me in line and to do me and others good, I'll delight in all the other difficulties You send my way, too, knowing they'll do me nothing but good." (See verses 9-10.)

Yes, we truly can trust God in all things to do us only eternal good. This trust, when accompanied by quiet waiting on God, produces a peace and rest of heart, mind, and spirit that leads to an increasing harmony of spirit with God—and, frequently, to a surprising degree of harmony with others.

Chapter 21

The Fallacy of Feelings

The testing of your faith produces patience....If any of
you lacks wisdom, let him ask of God, who gives to
all liberally and without reproach....But let him
ask in faith, with no doubting.
—James 1:3, 5–6

T he great enemy of faith and of spiritual growth
is feelings. The sweeping nature of this statement may surprise you. You may even want to
disagree. But I suspect that before we're done, you
might think this statement is true after all.

I hurt for all those who've never been taught the
basics of the spiritual life. But I hurt even more for
all those who, having been taught something of the
spiritual basics, have been sidetracked, their growth
in the Lord inhibited, their walk with God endan-
gered by their feelings.

Some Try to Live on an Emotional High

Today, as never before, there is a multitude of
people who are mistaking the good feelings worked
up in the fellowship of believers for the working faith
of the spiritual walk. They don't know and live the

143

spiritual basics. They live like leeches on the good feelings generated by the Christian crowd and augmented by the crowd's continued excitement about God, church, and ministry. They've never learned to walk with God in humble trust when surrounded by darkness. And when God "lets them down," when their most earnest prayers go unanswered, they fall apart. Some of them leave the church. Others hang in there hurting. Many pretend nothing has changed, when for them everything has changed. They live a lie.

The Devil's Tool

Even for those of us whose walk with God has not been initially based on feelings, but on a living, practical, moment-by-moment relationship with Him, the Devil uses our feelings to trip us up, mislead us, and deceive us in a virtually endless variety of ways.

When the Lord allows us to have delightful experiences with Him in prayer, we fall in love with the feelings more than with God. When the feelings dissolve, as they certainly will, we miss them so. We hurt, and we get angry with God for having run away and hid on us. Many of us never recover. We who thought the wonderful feelings of God's presence were a sign of spiritual maturity on our part, may end up living the rest of our lives in spiritual infancy, forever complaining, at least inwardly, about God's unfair treatment of us.

When we begin our Christian walk, we may learn something of worshiping God. We may revel in its privileges and benefits. We may enjoy it and the peace it tends to bring. Then our worship grows stale. We feel like the repetition of the words of worship is hypocritical, phony. We feel we don't mean them as we think we remember once meaning them.

We thought we were learning to rest in the Lord, only to watch the experienced rest flee, and our usual hurry, flurry, and worry return. We resent this. And returning moment by moment to the Lord to find our rest in Him is too much like work. Besides, our efforts don't always work out, so we give up.

More of His Tricks

We thought we were growing in the Lord, learning to live in victory and to walk with God in love. But we've become discouraged because none of our walk is the way we thought or hoped it would be. We once learned to practice immediate repentance and confession of our sins once they came to our attention. We once learned to confess, not only to God, but also to the people we sinned against. Now we feel that if we did confess our wrongdoing, we would be insincere. We don't feel that we want to repent.

We thought we had learned to walk with God one minute at a time. We thought we knew that the secret to spiritual victory isn't some great experience as much as turning to God constantly in every need, every temptation, every sin, every failure, yes, even in every blessing and every joy. But turning to God has become an effort instead of the delight we think we recall it once being.

To these scenarios we could add so many other instances in which we give in to our feelings and lose out directly as a result!

What Has Changed?

What has really changed? Perhaps nothing but our feelings! Oh, it's certainly possible we've backslidden. It's possible we've stopped spending sufficient time with the Lord in worship prayer. It's possible we've returned to centering our attention on ourselves instead of on God. It's very possible that at some particular point of obedience we've refused to die to our own desires in order to live for the Lord and His desires, and this choice has led to a general backslidden state.

But, even so, which came first—giving in to our feelings or backsliding? Which is the cause and which is the result? Perhaps the problem isn't so much that we backslid and then started giving in to our feelings as it is that we started giving in to our feelings first, living by them, and, as a result, backslid.

What Needs to Be Done about It?

In either case, what can be done about it? What can change your awful unhappiness, despondency, or depression into a joyous happiness of mind and spirit that supersedes all the difficulties of life?

First, recognize that God hasn't changed and the truths about the Christian life haven't changed. All is the same. Whatever your feelings, the facts remain the same. You must forsake living by your flighty feelings and return to living by the rock-firm facts of faith.

Second, you need to see that living by feelings instead of by faith is as impermissible a sin as any other.

Third, acknowledge that you can't cure the situation; you can't turn it around. Only the Lord can. Tell Him so. Ask Him to begin to cure it. Ask Him to give you the patience that will be so necessary if you are to allow Him to turn the situation around in His time and way. Give Him permission to change you the hard way if you prove unwilling to let Him change you the easy way. Be grateful, if not surprised, whenever He's able to work His divine work in you the easy way, without a great deal of suffering.

Fourth, remember that God has committed Himself to you and to the work needed in your spirit.

Being confident of this very thing, that He who has begun a good work in you will complete it until the day of Jesus Christ. (Phil. 1:6)

Remember that you must trust Him to be constantly doing that work no matter how little He seems to be doing it, no matter how undesirable to the flesh His methods may be, or how painful. Remember that a million years from now the suffering will seem negligible and the rewards massive.

Fifth, recognize that the reason we give in to our feelings instead of living in faith in God and His promises is, more than anything else, our prideful, fleshly rebellion, resistance, and resentment at what God permits in our lives. If, instead, we would accept the unacceptable as God's perfect will for us to purge and refine us and to make us like Him—if we would let go of our anger; relinquish our rebellion, resistance, and resentment; and rest contentedly in Him and whatever He wants for us—we would find new possibilities in living by faith instead of feelings. We would lay a wonderful foundation for renewed growth in God.

Sixth, seek God's grace to turn to Him in every circumstance. In particular, turn to Him every time you recognize that you're living and acting under the control of your feelings rather than under the control of His Word, His will, His person, and His promises. Simply recognize your need for Him to act on your behalf—all the way from making it possible for you to turn to Him to making it possible for you to depend on Him instead of yourself. He will also make it possible for you to forsake your feelings in order to trust in Him and His facts of faith. He will enable you to leave your rebellion, resistance, and resentment at what He allows in your life. He will restore your rest and contentment in Him in whatever circumstances He permits.

Seventh, DIE! Let God make you willing to die to your flesh, your pride, your way, your feelings, your independence, your self. Furthermore, live to Him. (See Romans 6:11.) There's no other way to live in newness of life in Him in the moment-by-moment walk of faith. None.

Christ is your hope and your life (Col. 3:4). If He is your Savior, you are in Him, and He is in you. Be glad of every reminder to die to yourself and to live in Him. Be glad for every reminder to turn to Him and see Him and respond to Him as all He really is to you.

Chapter 22

Never Give Up!

*I have set the LORD always before me; because He is
at my right hand I shall not be moved. Therefore my
heart is glad, and my glory rejoices; my flesh also will
rest in hope....You will show me the path of life; in
Your presence is fullness of joy; at Your right
hand are pleasures forevermore.*
—Psalm 16:8–9, 11

A re you unhappy? Are you no closer to being happy in Jesus than you were when you started your search? Do you feel, perhaps, further away?

Many of God's seeking saints search after more of the Lord for years without finding what they're looking for. Or, having once found something of what they were looking for, they now feel that they've lost it. Rightly or wrongly, they feel, not closer to Him, but further away from Him.

They may look enviously at those who experience emotional and temporal blessings, but still, deep inside, they long simply for a deeper, sweeter, more submissive walk with God.

They may be doing things they feel the Lord doesn't want them to do. They may lay them aside for a while, only to find themselves indulging again to their dismay, disgust, and disappointment.

Beginning to Give Up

After a time, they may begin to feel they'll never win, or, on the other hand, they may begin to think that perhaps these questionable practices aren't so wrong after all. They may quit fighting them. After all, what's the use?

They may spend less time with the Lord, and the time they do spend alone with Him in private prayer may seem less helpful than it once did. It seems as if they're talking to themselves, that God has taken a vacation, that He just isn't there for them. Now they're on the verge of entirely giving up their quest for more of God. What an awful position to be in!

Turn to the Lord

If you're in a position such as I've just described, you may try many ways to find help. But remember that good things will happen only to the extent that God is first...and you, not just second, but NOTHING, nothing but the recipient of His love and His love-gifts, from the moment of your conception in your mother's womb until you're with Him and like Him eternally.

Yes, you can ask Him for direction, guidance, correction, encouragement. You can give Him the right to do anything in your life that He needs to do to accomplish what He wants to accomplish. If you can't yet give Him this permission, you can ask Him to make you genuinely willing. His work is for your eternal benefit.

Start Rebuilding Your Time with Him

You may write or type your prayer thoughts to Him. Ask Him to enable you to be really honest with Him. Don't spare yourself, even if you'd be badly embarrassed to have anyone read what you write.

Learn to worship Him with words. Or, if you once knew how, return to the practice. Worship Him, praise Him, and give Him thanks. Allow Him to transform you at least a little more into the likeness of His perfection.

But remember that your primary purpose is to have your focus shifted from yourself and the things of time and space to the God of Glory. If anything you do keeps your attention for very long on yourself, it's counterproductive. Only what gets your attention off yourself and onto the Lord will bring you into the intimacy that you seek with Him, along with true and lasting peace and joy.

Our first tendency is to make commitments to God about what we will do and what we won't do. We've all done this repeatedly, only to end up in repeated failure. Another tendency is to condemn ourselves, live in constant guilt, and feel quite self-righteous in our self-condemnation. After all, we must be quite good to see how bad we are! In this state, prayer and Bible reading tend to produce only more self-condemnation, pain, and isolation from the God whom we've grieved.

There's only one ultimate answer: to look to the Lord, not ourselves. Rest in Him, trust in Him, rejoice in Him, wait quietly before Him, be with Him in peace and joy, worship Him in contentment and thanksgiving.

What about Our Failures?

This doesn't mean that we ignore our sins and failures altogether. No chance. The Spirit within us doesn't permit that. Of those things that aren't sins in themselves but remain causes of concern in our hearts and consciences, Romans 14:23 says, *"Whatever is not from faith is sin."* We won't have the peace of God reigning in our hearts until either the Lord shows us that our consciences have been unnecessarily disturbed, we stop engaging in the bothersome activities, or we look from our imperfections to the perfect God in whose righteousness we live.

Some habits may have such a stranglehold on us that it seems we're simply unable to finally let them go. If we're not careful, we'll ultimately give up trying to walk with the Lord in the intimacy we seek.

So, it's no light matter that you never give up seeking the Lord and worshiping Him.

Surprise!

But there's another sense in which the most helpful thing you could ever do is to give up. Give up any hope of your ever winning such terrible battles. If at last you come to the place where you're absolutely without hope, you'll finally be in the only place where there is hope.

Without knowing it, we secretly hope in ourselves. We say that we rely on the Lord, that only He can give us victory. But deep inside there are still hidden hopes that are founded, not on our absolute inability and God's exclusive ability, but somehow on something we can do. If our spiritual transformation arises from anything short of God Himself, we have something for which we may take credit. And God will have no part of this. He will not share His glory with another!

The Hopeless Case

The sooner you're pronounced a hopeless case, the better. With God, nothing is too hard; nothing is impossible (Luke 1:37). We never need to give up hope in what He can do, what He is willing to do, what He will do just as soon as it is safe for Him to do it, just as soon as all hope in ourselves is ripped from us and replaced by Him alone.

Again and again, it is God only, God ever, God always. Yes, it is GOD!

Chapter 23

Of Sacrifice and Suffering

*He who loves father or mother more than Me is not
worthy of Me. And he who loves son or daughter more
than Me is not worthy of Me. And he who does not
take his cross and follow after Me is not worthy of Me.
He who finds his life will lose it, and he who loses
his life for My sake will find it.*
—Matthew 10:37–39

What or who comes first in your life? No matter where you are, unless God comes first, you're in trouble. You were made that way, for God to be first. And, to the extent that's not the way it is, nothing's really right. You can try to find answers to your anger, anxiety, fear, frustration, worry, depression, peevishness, hopelessness, or any other emotional or spiritual problem. You may certainly find help, but you'll not find an ultimate solution.

God's way is always the way of the cross!

What would you say if God asked you to give up your job and serve Him in full-time ministry on faith alone? What if He asked you to stop seeing your girlfriend or boyfriend? To stop watching television entirely? To give up your music? To prepare for the ministry? To give all of your income to Him except what is necessary for essential bodily needs? To serve God where you are certain to suffer severe persecution? To give up a particular friendship? To move out of your fine home into something much less expensive and to give the money to Him? To stop smoking, drinking alcoholic beverages, or overeating? To give up your vacation, your position in the community, or the respect of your fellow men? To forsake that favorite hidden sin? To confess publicly the grossest act of sin of your life? To...well, you fill in the rest!

What if He is asking you to trust Him, even to the extent of becoming a martyr for Him? What is your answer? If it isn't an unequivocal yes and martyrdom becomes a genuine possibility, obviously you'll not be able to be at peace with Him. You'll not find answers for your troubled soul and spirit.

The question here is, What do you covet more than communion with God and fellowship with Christ? Such covetousness is said in Colossians 3:5 to be *"idolatry,"* which is placing something, anything, ahead of God in your affection.

No matter how difficult it may seem, you need to make it your aim to love God with all your heart, soul, mind, and strength (Mark 12:30). Let Him be first!

Now, let me walk you through the pages of the New Testament and give you an entirely new picture of what being a Spirit-filled, victorious Christian deeply in love with Christ really means—what it has always meant.

It means being willing to agree with the Holy Spirit when He tells us we must be prepared with the apostle Paul to go the way of the cross, to suffer the deprivation of all things.

It means willingly giving up something at the least pressure of the Holy Spirit on our spirits.

It means denying ourselves, suffering with Christ, and falling to the ground and dying to ourselves (John 12:24–25).

It means becoming part of His redemptive work in us and in others, not by gaining merit or by outward service, but by the transforming power of divinely appointed sacrifice.

It means being gladly crucified with Christ (Gal. 2:20) so that we may take part with Him in *"bringing many sons to glory"* (Heb. 2:10).

Peter made some shocking statements in this connection in 1 Peter.

> *For to this you were called, because Christ also suffered for us, leaving us an example, that you should follow His steps...who Himself bore our sins in His own body on the tree, that we, having died to sins, might live for righteousness.*
> *(1 Pet. 2:21, 24)*

> *Therefore, since Christ suffered for us in the flesh, arm yourselves also with the same mind.*
> *(1 Pet. 4:1)*

Jesus said,

> *If anyone desires to come after Me, let him deny himself, and take up his cross, and follow Me.* *(Matt. 16:24)*

> *Unless a grain of wheat falls into the ground and dies, it remains alone; but if it dies, it*

produces much grain. He who loves his life will lose it, and he who hates his life in this world will keep it for eternal life.
(John 12:24–25)

So likewise, whoever of you does not forsake all that he has cannot be My disciple.   (Luke 14:33)

The apostle Paul, continuing the theme, declared,

I beseech you therefore, brethren, by the mercies of God, that you present your bodies a living sacrifice...which is...reasonable.   (Rom. 12:1)

For if you live according to the flesh you will die; but if by the Spirit you put to death the deeds of the body, you will live.   (Rom. 8:13)

We suffer with Him, that we may also be glorified together. For I consider that the sufferings of this present time are not worthy to be compared with the glory which shall be revealed in us.   (Rom. 8:17–18)

For we who live are always delivered to death for Jesus' sake, that the life of Jesus also may be manifested in our mortal flesh. (2 Cor. 4:11)

Even though our outward man is perishing, yet the inward man is being renewed day by day. For our light affliction, which is but for a moment, is working for us a far more exceeding and eternal weight of glory, while we do not look at the things which are seen, but at the things which are not seen. For the things

*which are seen are temporary, but the things
which are not seen are eternal. (2 Cor. 4:16–18)*

Does all this talk of persecution, suffering, and
affliction come as a shock to you? Well, this is
scarcely the beginning.

The writer to the Hebrews did one better in
shock value when he said,

*Therefore we also, since we are surrounded by
so great a cloud of witnesses, let us lay aside
every weight, and the sin which so easily en-
snares us, and let us run with endurance the
race that is set before us, looking unto Jesus,
the author and finisher of our faith, who for
the joy that was set before Him endured the
cross, despising the shame, and has sat down
at the right hand of the throne of God. For
consider Him who endured such hostility from
sinners against Himself, lest you become weary
and discouraged in your souls. You have not
yet resisted to bloodshed, striving against sin.*
(Heb. 12:1–4)

*See that you do not refuse Him who speaks....
For our God is a consuming fire.*
(Heb. 12:25, 29)

*Therefore Jesus also, that He might sanctify
the people with His own blood, suffered outside
the gate. Therefore let us go forth to Him, outside the camp, bearing His reproach. For here
we have no continuing city, but we seek the one
to come. (Heb. 13:12–14)*

Michael Molinos (1627–?), in his work *The Spiritual Guide,* said,

> You should have no desire for what will come out of your having an inward walk with God. Your desire must be to end your life for His sake. The way of your Lord was not sweetness and softness. And He never invited you, or anyone, into such a thing. The believer who would be united with Christ must follow Him in the way of suffering....What happiness of happinesses it is to be crucified with Christ....There is no higher honor than to be denied, to be despised, and to be crucified with Christ. Many do launch out into the inward way....Only a few come to the end of its path...because there are few who embrace the cross.

In addition, Paul said,

> *If then you were raised with Christ, seek those things which are above, where Christ is, sitting at the right hand of God. Set your mind on things above, not on things on the earth. For you died, and your life is hidden with Christ in God. When Christ who is our life appears, then you also will appear with Him in glory. Therefore put to death your members which are on the earth: fornication, uncleanness, passion, evil desire, and covetousness, which is idolatry.*
> *(Col. 3:1–5)*

> *And whatever you do, do it heartily, as to the Lord and not to men, knowing that from the*

Lord you will receive the reward of the inheritance; for you serve the Lord Christ.
                    (Col. 3:23–24)

Paul gave his personal testimony in these words:

But what things were gain to me, these I have counted loss for Christ. Yet indeed I also count all things loss for the excellence of the knowledge of Christ Jesus my Lord, for whom I have suffered the loss of all things, and count them as rubbish, that I may gain Christ...that I may know Him and the power of His resurrection, and the fellowship of His sufferings, being conformed to His death, if, by any means, I may attain to the resurrection from the dead.
                    (Phil. 3:7–8, 10–11)

For many walk, of whom I have told you often, and now tell you even weeping, that they are the enemies of the cross of Christ: whose end is destruction, whose god is their belly, and whose glory is in their shame; who set their mind on earthly things. For our citizenship is in heaven, from which we also eagerly wait for the Savior, the Lord Jesus Christ....Therefore, my beloved and longed-for brethren, my joy and crown, so stand fast in the Lord, beloved....I know how to be abased, and I know how to abound. Everywhere and in all things I have learned both to be full and to be hungry, both to abound and to suffer need. I can do all things through Christ who strengthens me.
                    (Phil. 3:18–20; 4:1, 12–13)

I have been crucified with Christ; it is no longer I who live, but Christ lives in me; and the life which I now live in the flesh I live by faith in the Son of God, who loved me and gave Himself for me. (Gal. 2:20)

And those who are Christ's have crucified the flesh with its passions and desires. If we live in the Spirit, let us also walk in the Spirit. (Gal. 5:24–25)

Do not be deceived, God is not mocked; for whatever a man sows, that he will also reap. For he who sows to his flesh will of the flesh reap corruption, but he who sows to the Spirit will of the Spirit reap everlasting life. And let us not grow weary while doing good, for in due season we shall reap if we do not lose heart. (Gal. 6:7–9)

But God forbid that I should boast except in the cross of our Lord Jesus Christ, by whom the world has been crucified to me, and I to the world. (Gal. 6:14)

I bear in my body the marks of the Lord Jesus. (Gal. 6:17)

I now rejoice in my sufferings for you, and fill up in my flesh what is lacking in the afflictions of Christ, for the sake of His body, which is the church. (Col. 1:24)

To this end I also labor, striving according to His working which works in me mightily. (Col. 1:29)

Let this mind be in you which was also in Christ Jesus, who, being in the form of God, did not consider it robbery to be equal with God, but made Himself of no reputation, taking the form of a bondservant, and coming in the likeness of men. And being found in appearance as a man, He humbled Himself and became obedient to the point of death, even the death of the cross.   *(Phil. 2:5–8)*

Madame Jeanne Guyon (1648–1717) said,

You will not find consolation in anything other than love of the cross and total abandonment. If you will not savor the cross, you cannot savor the things of God, as it is impossible to love God without loving the cross. If you savor the cross, you will find even the most bitter things to be sweet. God gives us the cross, and the cross gives us God. Abandonment and the cross go hand in hand....Give yourself and your circumstances to Him in sacrifice....If you sincerely love God, you will love all that belongs to Him.

We are told in Ephesians,

Awake, you who sleep....Walk circumspectly, not as fools but as wise, redeeming the time, because the days are evil. Therefore do not be unwise, but understand what the will of the Lord is.   *(Eph. 5:14–17)*

Where is easy-going Christianity? Where is carnal fundamentalism? Where is the grasping "word of faith"? Where is positive-thinking Christianity? Where is prosperity teaching? Where are the minister's mansions? Where is evangelical salesmanship? NOT HERE!

> *Then a certain scribe came and said to Him [Jesus], "Teacher, I will follow You wherever You go." And Jesus said to him, "Foxes have holes and birds of the air have nests, but the Son of Man has nowhere to lay His head."*
> *(Matt. 8:19–20)*

> *Jesus said to Simon Peter, "Simon, son of Jonah, do you love Me more than these [bread and fish]?"...And when He [Jesus] had spoken this, He said to him [Peter], "Follow Me."*
> *(John 21:15, 19)*

To follow Jesus is ever the way of the cross. Will you follow anywhere He leads? Or will you put a limit on His leading, refuse to die to your own desires, and set up your own idols and worship them more than the Christ of the cross, even while loudly proclaiming your love for Him?

Paul said in 1 Corinthians,

> *For I think that God has displayed us, the apostles, last, as men condemned to death; for we have been made a spectacle to the world, both to angels and to men. We are fools for Christ's sake....We are weak....We are dishonored! To the present hour we both hunger and thirst, and we are poorly clothed, and beaten, and homeless. And we labor, working with our*

*own hands. Being reviled, we bless; being per-
secuted, we endure; being defamed, we entreat.
We have been made as the filth of the world,
the offscouring of all things until now....
Therefore I urge you, imitate me.*

(1 Cor. 4:9–13, 16)

Teresa of Avila (1515–1582) said,

There are many who begin and yet who
never reach the end. I believe that this is due
largely to a failure to embrace the cross from
the beginning.

Chapter 24

The Martyr

I say to you, My friends, do not be afraid of those
who kill the body, and after that have
no more that they can do.
—Luke 12:4

During the past century, Christians in much of the world have entertained the idea that persecution of Christians even to the death has become a thing of the past. Of course, it hasn't. In many countries it is still not safe to be a Christian. There, martyrdom is the rule rather than the exception.

As we've just seen, the New Testament is full of warnings to expect to be persecuted even to the death. But we need not fear. God will be with us even in death. And death is only a prelude to glorious, wonderful, perfect, flawless, joyous eternal life.

If God is for us, who can be against us? He
who did not spare His own Son, but delivered
Him up for us all, how shall He not with Him
also freely give us all things?...Who shall
separate us from the love of Christ? Shall
tribulation, or distress, or persecution, or

167

famine, or nakedness, or peril, or sword? As it is written: "For Your sake we are killed all day long; we are accounted as sheep for the slaughter." Yet in all these things we are more than conquerors through Him who loved us. For I am persuaded that neither death nor life, nor angels nor principalities nor powers, nor things present nor things to come, nor height nor depth, nor any other created thing, shall be able to separate us from the love of God which is in Christ Jesus our Lord.   *(Rom. 8:31–32, 35–39)*

Paul and the other apostles lived in daily danger of death at the hands of the enemies of the Gospel. In 1 Corinthians 15:30, Paul said that his life was *"in jeopardy every hour."*

It seems that most of the apostles and many other early church leaders died as martyrs. James, the brother of John, was beheaded. Bartholomew, after preaching in India, was beaten and crucified in Armenia. Simon, the son of Mary Cleophas, was crucified in Egypt. Andrew was crucified. Matthew was speared in Africa. Jesus' brother James was thrown from the temple, stoned, and finally bludgeoned. Peter was crucified upside down at Rome. Paul was decapitated at Rome.

In Hebrews 11, the great faith chapter, the stories of a few of the great characters of faith are told, culminating with a number of general allusions to marvelous achievements of faith. These conclude with, *"Women received their dead raised to life again"* (Heb. 11:35).

Then the chapter continues:

Others were tortured, not accepting deliverance, that they might obtain a better resurrection. Still others had trial of mockings and scourgings, yes, and of chains and imprisonment. They were stoned, they were sawn in two, were tempted, were slain with the sword. They wandered about in sheepskins and goatskins, being destitute, afflicted, tormented; of whom the world was not worthy. They wandered in deserts and mountains, in dens and caves of the earth. (Heb. 11:35–38)

This description ends with, *"And all these...obtained a good testimony through faith"* (v. 39).

Some lived in faith. Some died by faith. And God honored them all equally.

I read *Foxe's Book of Martyrs* when I was still a youngster. It left an indelible mark on my life. I knew that to really be a Christian, I needed to be willing to follow Christ even to the death.

If you've never read that book, get a copy and read it today.* Of course, if, for whatever reason, reading it would only cause you to be worried and fearful, rather than to trust and rest in God, it would be unwise to do so. Just commit your way to the Lord, and ask Him to enable you to trust Him and stand true to Him, whatever the future may hold.

We would be well advised to prepare our hearts, minds, and spirits to look squarely at the possibility that we might be called upon to die a martyr's death.

---

* John Foxe, *Foxe's Book of Martyrs* (New Kensington, PA: Whitaker House, 1981).

However, God will never leave us or forsake us (Heb. 13:5). He will never ask us to suffer more than we can endure.

And we have something gloriously exciting to look forward to. We may shortly leave this vale of tears, exchanging it for eternal ease and perfection in unlimited, joyous fellowship with our God and Savior. In heaven, there'll be nothing to mar the bliss that will be ours with Him evermore.

> *For I consider that the sufferings of this present time are not worthy to be compared with the glory which shall be revealed in us.*
> *(Rom. 8:18)*

Not only should we be prepared to face possible martyrdom, but we need to be ready to help others who might be tempted to turn their backs on the Lord if they do not have others who are better prepared than they are to encourage them.

And if the Lord calls us home without our having to suffer martyrdom, I believe this attitude of willingness to be a martyr will have helped us live a life of constant dying to ourselves and our selfish desires in order to live in the life of Christ (Rom. 6:11).

May the Lord enable us to live as martyrs minute by minute of every day remaining to us.

This is real living!

Chapter 25

The Wonders of Joy in Suffering

Rejoice in the Lord always. Again I will say, rejoice!...Be anxious for nothing, but in everything by prayer and supplication, with thanksgiving, let your requests be made known to God; and the peace of God, which surpasses all understanding, will guard your hearts and minds through Christ Jesus.
—Philippians 4:4, 6–7

As we have seen, the Bible has much to say about the Christian's response to suffering and death. The following verses remind us further of God's truth on this matter:

> *For our light affliction, which is but for a moment, is working for us a far more exceeding and eternal weight of glory, while we do not look at the things which are seen, but at the things which are not seen. For the things which are seen are temporary, but the things which are not seen are eternal. (2 Cor. 4:17–18)*

> *It is good for me that I have been afflicted, that I may learn Your statutes.   (Ps. 119:71)*

> *I do not want you to be ignorant, brethren, concerning those who have fallen asleep, lest you*

171

sorrow as others who have no hope....Therefore comfort one another with these words.

(1 Thess. 4:13, 18)

Are Christians Really Different?

I sat in a discussion group. The topic was death and the pain associated with it. It was a Christian group; however, as the session moved along, I was struck by the extent to which the treatment of the subject was so like the way Christless people who have no hope of heaven might treat it. It was as though the people in the group needed to prove that they were human, too...as though they needed to prove that they were in touch with reality by showing that they suffer the same way Christless people suffer.

Just look at the Christless people around you. Are they able to live happily when their world falls apart? They can't. They don't have the wherewithal!

Do We Really Have to Respond As the Ungodly Respond?

This was by no means the first time I'd been struck by the way Christians try to deal with suffering on the same basis as the unconverted.

I once read a book that seemed to be written not only as the story of one person's effort to deal with the threat and ultimate reality of a parent's death, but also to help others who go through the same kind of agony. While there were ways and times that the author got help from God, the basic perception of how to deal with pain seemed, to me at least, to be very humanistic.

I'm sure many who have read this chapter up to this point will already be wanting to warn me against the danger of not dealing realistically and thoroughly with death and dying and other forms of human agony.

Spiritual Christians Are First of All Realists!

It's foolish indeed to pretend that, in the face of difficult circumstances, a believer does not experience fear, anxiety, hurt, pain, separation, deprivation, loneliness, guilt, suffering, and agony much as those do who don't know Christ. Hundreds of situations breed these problems in the human heart and life. These situations are very real and absolutely inescapable.

Has Christianity Nothing More?

But, unless we have something more than this to say about threatening, hurtful, and painful situations, we admit that our Christianity has little practical help for its adherents. We admit that it claims more than it can actually produce. We are saying that there's no way it can make a person happy when his world falls apart around him.

This is the distressing truth of the matter for those content with a carnal Christianity that has in it little of the divine, little of the life of the Spirit.

But this is not the New Testament Christianity that pervades every detail of life with a vibrancy that is inescapable; that changes absolutely everything it

173

is allowed to impact freely; that replaces unrest, anxiety, pain, and human misery with a peace that passes all understanding (Phil. 4:7).

How we react in every difficult situation is determined in large measure by where our hearts and spirits are in our everyday lives before we are faced with the dreadful circumstance. But it is also true that our response in each particular circumstance is significantly affected by how our minds have been pretrained to respond to the circumstance—what we think is expected of us, what we see as appropriate and inappropriate.

Be Careful What You Buy Into

If we have come to believe the psychologists, psychiatrists, sociologists, and "great" minds of this world more than the Word of God enlivened by His Spirit, we will deal with the difficult circumstances of this life only as unbelieving humans do.

But if, against all human wisdom, we accept in our hearts and spirits what the divinely enlivened Word of God shows us to be true, we will benefit wonderfully from the release, joy, and liberty that is brought to those who live in and enjoy the freedom of spiritual reality.

Know the Limitlessly Magnificent Difference

We will benefit from a perception of reality that is not limited to the human but is open to the spiritual, the infinite, the eternal. We can choose to live in the dimension of the human or that of the divine

Spirit, and suffer or enjoy accordingly. We can choose to rest in God or dwell on our misfortune. Oh, what a limitlessly magnificent difference!

Yes, It Does Work in Real Life

The day after the discussion group session that I referred to at the beginning of this chapter, I got this letter:

> Thank you for this pamphlet, "Let Go and Let God." I was having trouble with my son and was all upset. Its message put my mind at ease and helped my husband greatly, too. Then, last week, I lost my dear friend to cancer. The pamphlet helped me to focus on God's will, not mine, and brought peace to my heart because God has taken her to a much better place.

A very dear friend faxed me the following letter:

> My husband didn't understand my pain, and I almost "lost it." So I came into my prayer closet and used the Golden Key again that you spoke about in your book (*A Christianity That Really Works*). It is so profound: Withdraw from things outward to rest in Him.
>
> Just moments ago, I told the Lord, "I feel uncomfortable. Help me, in spite of all the reasons I have to be ill at ease, to be at peace in You." I worshiped Him, repeating many of His characteristics to Him. In minutes the tears began to flow, and His peace settled on my heart. Then He immediately removed two of the causes of discomfort. Praise Him.

We Don't Have to Suffer Like Those Who Have No Hope Unless We Choose To

For us, the divine, eternal, infinite, spiritual realities can far exceed the human realities—no matter how overwhelmingly inescapable the human realities at first may seem to be.

As God's people turn from themselves and their pain to God and His infinite supply, the hurting find comfort, the lonely find fellowship, the unhappy find joy, the fearful find confidence, the weary find rest, the overburdened find peace.

Let us not respond to the trials, difficulties, pains, and sorrows of this life as the unconverted respond. Let us not approach either life or death as they do, but as He does.

The difference will be incredibly blessed. All glory to God!

Chapter 26

When God Can't Be Trusted

But without faith it is impossible to please Him, for
he who comes to God must believe that He is, and that
He is a rewarder of those who diligently seek Him.
—Hebrews 11:6

There's no greater hindrance to being happy in Christ than mistrusting God. None. You can count on it!

Well then, why don't we actually trust Him when the chips are down? Because, in truth, we don't consider Him trustworthy. We really don't. We're afraid of what He'll ask of us, what He'll put us through, what He'll deprive us of, what He'll allow us to suffer.

Yes, in actual fact, we don't trust God. We don't consider Him trustworthy! We're afraid to place ourselves unreservedly in His hands.

Well now, we have a very simple choice. We can trust God, or we can not trust God. We can trust God, or we can trust ourselves. We can trust God, or we can trust someone or something else. God help us!

David said it for us:

Some trust in chariots, and some in horses; but
we will remember the name of the LORD our
God.   *(Ps. 20:7)*

God, through His prophet Isaiah, told a fearful later generation of David's people,

> *For thus says the Lord GOD, the Holy One of Israel: "In returning and rest you shall be saved; in quietness and confidence shall be your strength." But you would not, and you said, "No, for we will flee on horses"; therefore you shall flee! And, "We will ride on swift horses"; therefore those who pursue you shall be swift!...Blessed are all those who wait for Him.* (Isa. 30:15–16, 18)

Isaiah said to the people who would not wait trustingly for God,

> *When you cry out, let your collection of idols deliver you. But the wind will carry them all away, a breath will take them. But he who puts his trust in Me shall possess the land.*
> (Isa. 57:13)

So we really don't have a choice. To put our trust anywhere but in our wonderful Lord is to live in constant fear, frustration, and failure.

It's Trust God or Lose Out

So, from now on I'm going to trust God. It's as simple as that.

Sure it is!

Who are we kidding anyway?

That kind of thinking is at the root of our failure. We can't suddenly force ourselves to start trusting God—we who have developed an entrenched habit of not really trusting Him, all the while thinking that we are trusting Him. No. That's impossible. And we should recognize it to be such.

What Then?

A whole new attitude, a new outlook, a new viewpoint is needed. A heavenly mindset.

Now, that may really throw you a curve. You've probably bought the humanist line about being so heavenly-minded that you're no earthly good. Instead, as a matter of fact, it's when we become heavenly-minded that we are some earthly good.

> *Set your mind on things above, not on things on the earth. For you died, and your life is hidden with Christ in God.*   *(Col. 3:2–3)*

> *If then you were raised with Christ, seek those things which are above, where Christ is, sitting at the right hand of God.*   *(Col. 3:1)*

You see, it's right here that we have our really big problem. We think in terms of the human, the physical, the temporal. We're desperately limited in our perceptions as a result. We don't see as God sees, so we entirely misunderstand His workings, and we naturally learn to mistrust Him.

We read, *"All things work together for good to those who love God, to those who are the called according to His purpose"* (Rom. 8:28), and we expect our physical and temporal circumstances to immediately improve as a result. Instead, our circumstances may get even worse. We become confused and frustrated. We blame God. We find Him untrustworthy! He didn't keep His promise!

The Heavenly Look

What are the purposes to which He has called us? Are they not to know Him, to love Him, to worship Him, to be conformed to His image (Rom. 8:29), to glorify Him, and to enjoy Him forever?

Now, is immediately giving us all we want in the physical and temporal domain going to produce this glorious fruit?

No. He must prune and purge us before such heavenly fruit can be borne on His earthly branches. This purging and pruning is not without its pain. But, oh, what glorious pain, if only it forms the image of Christ in us!

Now, this new viewpoint will never be mine, nor will this glorious result of the pruning and purging— not until I give myself to seeking the Lord in His beauty above and to seeking what He has for me there in preference to what is here. Only in this way will I die to my self-centered earthly concerns and live for His eternal purposes for me. Only in this way will I begin to find Him ever and always in all things trustworthy. Glorious opportunity!

Chapter 27

"God Is...."

For of Him and through Him and to Him are all
things, to whom be glory forever. Amen.
—Romans 11:36

H ow could someone ever adequately describe
our vast God? Certainly, this is an impossible
task. However, I have written a poem entitled
simply "God Is...." It contains some of my thoughts
on the precious Father, Son, and Holy Spirit.

GOD IS GOD.

What can be added?

Perfect beyond measure.
Infinitely perfect. Perfectly infinite.
Eternally perfect. Perfectly eternal.
Perfectly holy. Wholly perfect.

Still, in His inviolable perfection
is no aloofness or snobbery.

Just perfect love.
Love that gives the best it has.

Love that hurts where no hurt should be,
because of the glad sacrifice of the Best Loved
for the least deserving.
Love that willingly accepts
neglect, scorn, hatred, and rejection
in anticipation that some who hate Him
will finally come to love and long for Him.

GOD IS GOD.

Perfect is He in every dimension.

Yet, truly Father,
He is infinitely tender and caring.
As infinite and eternal as He is,
He is infinitely interested in and concerned about
every need of His human creation.
He does not have any need,
nor can He ever have.
He is self-contained,
with perfectly selfless self-satisfaction.
Yet He chose to want and "need"
the fellowship and love
of people created in His own image.

GOD IS GOD.

What more can be said?

God is God by any name.
The rock of our salvation,
the God of hope,
the God of peace,
King of Kings,

Lord of Lords,
the Alpha and Omega,
the beginning and the end.

Faithful and true,
just and pure.
Totally trustworthy.
He keeps His promises,
even when it seems clearly otherwise,
working everything always
for our eternal benefit
and His everlasting praise.

Omnipotent,
omniscient,
and omnipresent,
He can do anything He wishes.
He knows everything there is to know,
and He is everywhere all the time.

GOD IS GOD.

Without fault or flaw,
He defies description.

When mortal man seeks words enough
to define or describe Him,
he finds himself entirely baffled.
He's left aching with an overwhelming sense
of absolute inadequacy and total bewilderment.

Whether man is seeking to describe Him,
to understand Him,
to know Him,

or to experience Him
makes no difference.
Man is still baffled and bewildered.
Not because God is hard to understand,
know,
or experience.
But because in His infinite perfection,
He is just too much for the human.
He is always more.

We're left longing
to know more, more, and yet more,
better, and forever yet better ways
to admiringly
view, experience, and describe
this infinitely perfect God.

GOD IS GOD.

Yet to know Him as He is,
is the deepest longing of the human heart.
Mostly unrecognized,
yet forever felt,
this longing is misappropriated,
misplaced,
as men seek madly for Something.

They know not what.
They know not why.
Still, they seek for Something,
rather, Someone.
Someone whose name is God!

GOD IS GOD.

184

Three persons, but one God.
Amazing Trinity.

The Savior/Son is
the Way,
the Truth,
the Life,
the Light of the World,
the Shepherd good and great,
the Door,
the Bread of Life,
the well of living water,
the precious one,
the bright and morning star,
the fairest of ten thousand,
the Prince of Peace,
Master,
Lord,
Redeemer,
Counselor,
Friend of sinners,
gracious and good.

The blessed Holy Spirit
seeks no place of special honor,
but points to the eternal Savior/Son.
Still, He is the operative Agent
in all the work of God
performed in and on behalf of
His human creation.
And, as such,
He deserves and draws forth
the unstinting worship and honor
owed all Three.

185

Father God.
Unseen. Unseeable.
Yet revealed in all of His magnificent creation,
boggling the mind with its infinite science.
And revealed still more in the living Word,
the Savior/Son.
Worthy is He of worship, praise,
adoration, honor, and love
beyond human expression
or human capacity.

GOD IS GOD.

May my heart be moved within me
to immeasurable depths of holy desire.
May I seek nothing,
desire nothing,
need nothing so much as God.
May all things else and less be unattractive
in comparison with God.
May the impossibility of words
to convey worship of so great a God
drive me to holy silence and awe
before the infinite One.
May my spirit be moved
to gratitude inexpressible
that Love won me,
blood bought me,
and grace saved me,
the chief of sinners,
forever undeserving,
but eternally forgiven and restored.

May my attention return quickly
from this glance at my sinful self
to rest forever on Him
who alone is worthy.
May He captivate my heart's affection
evermore.

GOD IS GOD.

FOREVER GOD.

Chapter 28

Our Hope Is in Him Alone

In [God] *are hidden all the treasures of wisdom and knowledge....And you are complete in Him, who is the head of all principality and power.*
—Colossians 2:3, 10

That God may be all in all.
—1 Corinthians 15:28

We may know the above verses very well, but often one of our greatest problems is a constant and increasing awareness of our sinful failure. We often feel so guilty, so wrong, so hurt, so sinful. We wonder why we're not making more spiritual progress, why we succumb to the same old temptations, why we can't live in uninterrupted victory.

For some of us, this problem leads to discouragement and despondency. For others, it leads to acceptance of failure as all we can ever hope for. What it should be doing is driving us to the Lord.

Misplaced Expectations

Why did we ever expect anything better of ourselves than sin and failure?

There is none righteous, no, not one.
(Rom. 3:10)

*If we say that we have no sin, we deceive our-
selves, and the truth is not in us.   (1 John 1:8)*

Yes, there is goodness for us. There is righteousness for us. There is spiritual victory for us. However, they plainly are not *in us*. They are in Christ
alone.

This thought once set the great missionary
leader Hudson Taylor on a quest to find out how we
get the victory that's in Christ out of Him!

We don't.

We take advantage of the magnificent reality
that Christ Himself is in us. It is not just His power,
His goodness, or even His life that is in us, but
Christ Himself is in us.

*God willed to make known what are the riches
of the glory of this mystery...which is **Christ
in you**, the hope of glory.*
(Col. 1:27, emphasis added)

Furthermore, we take advantage of the matching
magnificent reality that **we are in Christ**.

*[God] raised us up together, and made us sit
together in the heavenly places **in Christ Jesus**....For we are His workmanship, created **in
Christ Jesus** for good works.*
(Eph. 2:6, 10, emphasis added)

*I am the vine, you are the branches. He who
abides in Me, and I in him, bears much fruit;
for without Me you can do nothing.   (John 15:5)*

190

The source of the branch's life is the vine. It is vine life that works in the branch, causing it to bring forth fruit. The branch has absolutely no independent life.

Nor do we.

Christ...is our life. (Col. 3:4)

If it's goodness or righteousness or holiness or victory over sin that we need, we have it—not in ourselves, but in Christ, in God who lives in us, and in whom we live.

No one is good but One, that is, God.
                                          (Matt. 19:17)

I'm no good! You're no good!
God is good.
We're in Him. He's in us. And He has all we need, whether it's sanctification (holiness), wisdom, or anything else.

To God Be the Glory

But to allow His life to flow freely in us, freely supplying all we need, there is a prerequisite.

Not many wise according to the flesh, not many mighty, not many noble, are called. But God has chosen the foolish things of the world to put to shame the wise, and God has chosen the weak things of the world to put to shame the things which are mighty; and the base things of the world and the things which are

191

> *despised God has chosen, and the things which are not, to bring to nothing the things that are, that no flesh should glory in His presence. But of Him you are **in Christ Jesus**, who became for us wisdom from God; and righteousness and sanctification and redemption; that, as it is written, "He who glories, let him glory in the LORD."*   *(1 Cor. 1:26–31, emphasis added)*

God has said He will not give His glory to another. If we desire to have His life flowing freely in ours, bringing spiritual success in place of failure, we must be willing to let it be *His* life, *His* success, and *His* glory!

It's our place to humble ourselves to be nothing in order to let Him be Glorious Everything. There's absolutely no other way to be happy in the midst of discomfort, threats, and suffering.

> *Christ is all and in all.*   *(Col. 3:11)*

> *For of Him and through Him and to Him are all things, to whom be glory forever. Amen.*
> *(Rom. 11:36)*

Dying to Self

When we try to live the Christian life by our own abilities and efforts, if we could succeed, we would deserve the credit! But all we can achieve is failure. For that we deserve the credit, too.

All we're good for is to die.

> *I have been crucified with Christ; it is no longer I who live, but Christ lives in me; and*

*the life which I now live in the flesh I live by
faith in the Son of God, who loved me and
gave Himself for me.*   *(Gal. 2:20)*

When we received the Lord as our Savior, we
died with Christ to our old sin-dominated life. Therefore, we're no longer obligated to live under sin's
power. Now Christ lives in us with His own omnipotent, perfectly holy life.

It's our place to give Him our heart's attention
and love. It's our place to delightedly die to our
wishes and our glory—to all but Him. It's our place
to happily accept suffering and death as His way of
releasing His life in us. There's no other way to life
and happiness.

*What things were gain to me, these I have
counted loss for Christ....That I may know
Him and the power of His resurrection, and
the fellowship of His sufferings, being conformed to His death.*   *(Phil. 3:7, 10)*

Turning to God in Every Situation

We cannot give ourselves, our hearts, our time,
our interest, our affection to the things of this world
and at the same time live freely in Christ and have
Him live freely in us, His life flowing in us in spiritual power. We need to make Him our goal, our
hope, our life. We need to spend time with Him,
wait on Him, meditate on Him, abide in Him, set our
affection on Him. We need to trust Him, rely on Him,
depend on Him. We need to look, not to ourselves,
but to Him alone to receive from Him all we need.

We need to give ourselves constantly and with each new temptation or opportunity to seeking Him and His all-sufficiency, so that His life is released into that new situation. We seek Him this way for two reasons. One: we want to please Him and glorify His name. Two: we need Him, and we know we need Him.

Only God can please God. We'll never be able to please Him in our own strength. So we turn to Him to do the pleasing in each new circumstance.

The basis for our victory is not any effort of ours. None. It is the quiet assurance that He in us is all we can ever need. He is completely capable of handling absolutely every circumstance that may come our way. All we need to do is turn our attention away from ourselves and our circumstances, failures, and fears and rest quietly in Him and His all-encompassing capabilities.

To do anything less is to continue in our perpetual fear, frustration, and fretfulness.

Chapter 29

Glorious Failure!

Without Me you can do nothing.
—John 15:5

W e're sadly deceived if we think that by knowing spiritual truth we can live in the Spirit and become spiritually successful, happy, peaceful, and free. We're wrong if we think that merely with the passing of the years we may expect to become spiritual experts—knowing how to walk with God and be happy, free, and content in Him, and competently passing that knowledge on to others.

Spiritual maturity isn't that simple. Far from it! Accumulating religious knowledge, no matter how correct it may be, is no guarantee of spiritual success. If we depend on our religious knowledge, we become only more carnal, living more *"according to the flesh"* (Rom. 8:4) and less *"according to the Spirit"* (v. 4). Only by becoming and remaining poor and needy, dependent on God, can we achieve any spiritual growth. (See Matthew 5:3–6.) Only in this way can we live happily in Jesus regardless of life's circumstances.

Any minute that we're needy and heart-dependent on God, for that minute and to that extent, we're living in the Spirit, walking *"according to the Spirit."*

Any minute that we're self-dependent, forgetful of our great spiritual poverty and need, for that minute and to that extent, we're living in the flesh, walking *"according to the flesh,"* malcontent with our relationship with God and so with life.

Always in Everything

Our hope always needs to be in God—for everything in every circumstance during every minute.

If at any minute in anything I'm not actually poor and needy, the only reason is that in that moment and in that thing, God is replacing my need with His supply as I'm willingly dependent on Him.

In other words, there's never a time when I'm not poor and needy in the sense that I am dependent entirely on His supply. I must remember that in myself I can never be anything other than a failure spiritually. Better still, I must prefer to see myself as the failure that I am. It's only when I'm a willing failure that He can be my success.

Spiritual Poverty, the Way into God's Presence

When we come to Him in prayer, we don't truly come to Him at all unless we come as poor, needy, dependent failures, needing Him to be our success. Often we do not come this way, and herein lies the crux of much of our disappointment in prayer.

It's foolish to come to Him in prayer while our confidence, our trust, and our hope are in ourselves. Self-confidence is the death of prayer. Faith—trust in God—is the life of prayer. If our confidence, our trust, and our hope are even inadvertently in ourselves, they aren't in God, and no real prayer communion or exchange is going to take place. We can't worship God while, in fact, we're worshiping ourselves.

For Everyday Affairs, Too

This principle extends beyond the prayer life to all the everyday affairs of life. It's so easy to depend on ourselves, to look to ourselves rather than to God for the competence to handle the everyday matters that crowd the minutes and hours. Only when we come up against something that perplexes us do we tend to turn to the Lord for help.

Instead, we need to view our every circumstance as another opportunity to look to God to do through us all that needs to be done. Why must this be? Because there are factors in every circumstance that we don't see, know, or understand, all contributing hidden hindrances to the successful completion of any task.

Without Him, Nothing

More than this, we're obligated to acknowledge God in gratitude for the abilities that He has given us from birth. It's an offense to God for us to feel that we're capable of handling life's everyday circumstances by ourselves when we have nothing He has not given us, and when He, the omniscient, omnipotent, omnipresent God, is so lovingly willing to work for us. It should become an offense to us as well.

It should be our delight to be dependent on His help for all things, whether or not we see any special need for it, or foresee any special benefit for ourselves

197

from it. Instead, our deceitful hearts so often want to "go it alone." God forgive us.

It would be well, then, to ask God often for grace. On starting any task, however small, it would be wise to truly commit it to the Lord for His aid and to ask earnestly that we would be able to depend on Him for His enabling in it. On its completion, we should humbly thank Him for His intervention, empowering, and enabling. We would be greatly blessed, and God would be greatly honored.

Sometimes people are surprised that I so well understand their difficulties, failures, and needs. It's only because theirs are so often mine. I will give you one example.

While writing this chapter, I was also addressing several thousands of envelopes. From beginning to end, nothing seemed to go right, and in the morning someone would be waiting for them! Though I knew I should be depending on the Lord for the doing of that task, I simply wasn't. When finally, by His enabling, I genuinely committed the matter to Him for His intervention, the problems seemed to dissolve.

No, it isn't just the knowing that matters, as we've already said. God must enable the doing.

Our only glory is in Him—His grace and goodness...whether shown in creation, re-creation, transformation, or provision. The glory is all Him and His, now and forevermore.

> *Of Him and through Him and to Him are all things, to whom be glory forever. Amen.*
> *(Rom. 11:36)*

My wife keeps insisting this is my favorite verse. And why not?

Chapter 30

Every Day's a Wonderful Day

This is the day the LORD has made; we will
rejoice and be glad in it.
—Psalm 118:24

Every day is wonderful! It's wonderful because God is in charge, working everything together for our good (Rom. 8:28).

But I can hear you respond, "Sounds wonderful, brother. Preach it. But the facts are a little different. You're ignoring the pain and suffering, the disappointment and grief we experience."

No, as a matter of fact, I'm not ignoring them at all. I'm putting them in context. I'm putting them in the context of an almighty God whose business it is to see that nothing touches His children that doesn't bring them eternal benefit. Every bit of pain and suffering we'll ever know will all be sent by Him right on time and in the exact measure required for our eternal good. The omnipresent, omniscient, omnipotent, infinite, all-wise, and sovereign God is working in the realm of the realities of my sinful being, my human weakness, and my hurtful circumstances and is doing everything that can be done to bring me eternal benefit.

God Isn't Fazed by It All!

You ask, "What about fear, frustration, anxiety, and uncertainty?" Oh, yes, there'll be plenty of times in which we'll struggle with these in this life. But our God doesn't suffer from these things. He knows the end from the beginning. With Him, there's no uncertainty. Nor is there anything He can't handle. Nothing is too hard for Him. Nothing is ever out of His control. So how could He suffer from fear, frustration, anxiety, or uncertainty?

And, while I will experience them, it's a waste of time and effort! The One who is beyond their reach is working on everything that touches me so that I've no cause either for fear, frustration, anxiety, or uncertainty.

"Well then," you ask, "what about my having to experience deprivation, need, and lack?" First of all, we experience the fear of deprivation, need, and lack much more often than we actually experience the things themselves. We worry about having to do without the necessities of life a lot more than we have to do without them.

Second, we can never lack, for He has promised to supply all our need (Phil. 4:19). This being true, if He ever were to allow us to starve to death, then that would be what we needed! Of course, in most instances, starvation is not what God sees as our need, and He supplies our daily bread on schedule.

Still, it's wrong to assume that God always sees our needs as we see them. To be further reminded of this, read Hebrews 11 carefully to the end once more, or chapter 24 of this book.

We're One Day Nearer to Heaven

Now, even if we didn't understand and appreci-
ate this wonderful truth that God is fully in charge of
all our circumstances, working them all together for
our eternal benefit (Rom. 8:28), just one fact would
be enough to make every day a wonderful day. It is
this: we anticipate a gloriously perfect eternity with
nothing whatsoever to mar its perfection. Oh, may
we live every day between now and then, relishing
the hope of what God has laid up for you and me!

But, in the meantime, we want no make-believe,
no pretense. God is truth (John 14:6). So all He is, all
He gives, all He teaches must necessarily measure up
exactly to what actually is. To tell God's people to
praise Him for all their circumstances is to ask them
to be phony and unreal, unless they're taught first to
be truly thankful for the good God is doing in every
painful circumstance.

How Is It Possible?

The bottom line is a question of whether we're
willing to let God teach us to be more and more
grateful for His working all things for our benefit
(Rom. 8:28).

Or is it the bottom line? I've said it over and over
again (but can it be said too often?) that undergird-
ing our gratitude for God and His constant work on
our behalf is fundamental trust in God. He is omnipotent, omniscient, omnipresent, infinite, and eternal. He is perfect. He is perfectly capable, and He can
do no wrong. He's in charge of our affairs, personally
supervising them to bring eternal benefit from them.

Furthermore, what undergirds our trust is the long view, the eternal view, without which we see only the temporary suffering and not the eternal benefit. We're fools indeed to try to rejoice in the midst of the terrors and traumas of life if this life is all there is.

Yet most Christians, I honestly believe, live as though this life were it. We don't live with the long view in sight, where what is eternal and spiritual simply outweighs in value all that is temporal and physical.

Learning to Be at Home in God

To learn to trust God implicitly to bring benefit to us from all things, to learn to live with Him and all that is eternal and spiritual in view, we need to walk in fellowship with Him. We need to learn to live in communion, heart submission, and tenderness of spirit toward Him.

Unless we experience this kind of fellowship with Him in abundance, the things of this world will fill all our view, and not a thing I've written can make any sense. But flowing out from this tenderhearted communion with Him is rest and peace of heart and mind.

The thankfulness, the joy, and the rejoicing I've spoken of aren't the painstaking results of reasoning all of this through. They're the spontaneous results of God at work in our hearts and spirits in peace. All of these benefits spontaneously spring in turn from extensive time spent alone with God—learning to worship and praise Him for Himself alone, to rest in Him, to trust Him, to rely on Him, to live at home in

Him. There we learn not to be anxious in prayer, but to believe God simply, quietly, trustingly for all we actually, ultimately need.

This is prayer at its greatest effectiveness: simple trust in and reliance on almighty God, who is entirely capable and willing to act in every circumstance. I am talking about simple worship of our great God, simple resting at peace in Him. Glorious freedom! Wondrous joy!

People will forever try to rob you of this freedom and joy. They'll forever try to bring you back into *"bondage again to fear"* (Rom. 8:15). Know that this is the trick of the Devil. Flee to your refuge in Jesus. I've said it again and again, but here it is once more: rest there. Seek to remain always there, resting, trusting, communing in peace and quiet and utter dependence.

There may come a time in our lives when several times alone with the Lord throughout the day may be of greater value than a prolonged single period. On each occasion, we will release everything to God. The tears may flow; our hearts will become tender toward Him. Our spirits will be made gentle before Him. We'll let go of our resistance, resentment, and rebellion. We'll joy and rejoice in Him. We'll worship and praise, honor and glorify Him. We'll return to our abiding relationship of resting at home in God in peace, trust, and joy.

Yes, herein is freedom. Anything less is perpetual bondage to the terrors and traumas of temporal living.

Chapter 31

At Home in God

In Him [Christ]...*we have obtained an inheritance, being predestined according to the purpose of Him who works all things according to the counsel of His will, that we who first trusted in Christ should be to the praise of His glory....*[May you] *know what is the hope of His calling, what are the riches of the glory of His inheritance in the saints, and what is the exceeding greatness of His power toward us who believe, according to the working of His mighty power which He worked in Christ.*
—Ephesians 1:11–12, 18–20

My heart aches for the dear, sincere children of God who suffer because they don't please God as they feel He expects—or even because they don't live up to their own spiritual expectations. My heart aches because they suffer more the more sincere they are, the more they long to please the Lord and live up to their own expectations.

Fortunately, some of them know that they are *"accepted in the Beloved"* (Eph. 1:6), not because of their good behavior, but because of their place in Christ—not because of any righteousness of theirs, but because of the righteousness of the Lord Jesus

Christ, their Savior, that was placed freely to their account when they were totally and entirely unworthy.

Continued Suffering

Yet they continue to suffer because they don't love the Lord enough, they don't serve Him enough, they don't witness enough, they fail Him too often, they continue to sin even when they know better, they go back to Him over and over again confessing the same sin and feeling more and more guilty.

This problem does not affect everyone the same way. Some just go on day after day doing the best they can. Yes, they often feel guilty because they don't meet God's perfect standard, or, for that matter, their own imperfect standard. But, unlike those previously described, they feel there probably is nothing to be done about it; they're convinced that they're condemned to live in this kind of failure the rest of their lives.

Living in Law and Works

Neither one of these two groups sees that they are living in law and works, not in grace and faith.

It's our glorious privilege to be *"accepted in the Beloved"* (Eph. 1:6) in spite of our imperfections. We can live in our place in Christ, *"accepted in the Beloved."* We can live at home in the perfect righteousness of Christ that was imputed to us, placed to our account, when we first came to Him for forgiveness and salvation from our sin.

We can live, not content with our sins and imperfections, but content that, while we're told, *"Work out your own salvation with fear and trembling"* (Phil. 2:12), we're also told, *"It is God who works in you both to will and to do for His good pleasure"* (v. 13, emphasis added).

And while He is slowly but certainly working in us, we can be content with our place in Him. We can be satisfied with His righteousness, first placed to our account and then slowly but certainly worked in our spirits and worked out in our daily lives, as we seek Him and worship Him day by day.

The only alternative is to live according to our own self-righteous works. The only alternative is to live in constant disappointment and pain.

Many Aren't at Home Anywhere

I picked up the phone. The person at the other end was hurting. She felt like whatever she did wasn't good enough for those around her. Her husband wasn't dealing realistically with his emotions. He wouldn't talk through their problems.

And, as far as God was concerned, it seemed to be the same thing: she felt that she couldn't please Him either. She felt that He wasn't happy with her either.

Too many of us, as God's redeemed people, live so unnecessarily with this kind of pain. God has something better for us. This something better is, as always, Himself. This is not some abstract, indefinite concept that proves to be an impractical non-reality. It's very real and practical indeed!

Praise His name. We are in Him. He is in us. We are *"complete in Him"* (Col. 2:10). He fills us. We are dead to sin, alive with Christ to God and righteousness (Rom. 6:11). Our sins of the past are forgiven. Our present sins are all under the blood of Christ, for we confess and forsake the sins that we recognize.

> *If we walk in the light as He is in the light, we have fellowship with one another, and the blood of Jesus Christ His Son cleanses us from all sin....If we confess our sins, He is faithful and just to forgive us our sins and to cleanse us from all unrighteousness.* (1 John 1:7, 9)

> [We are] *accepted in the Beloved.* (Eph. 1:6)

> *He who has begun a good work in you will complete it until the day of Jesus Christ.* (Phil. 1:6)

In Practical Terms

What does all this mean in practical, everyday terms? It means that we can live at home with God— content, at ease, at peace, at rest in His love, His acceptance, and His enabling power. We don't have to live in self-condemnation and guilt.

In spite of our obvious imperfections, we can live in peace. We can live in contentment, not with ourselves or with anything about us, but with Him, what He has done for us, what He is doing for us, and what He is going to do for us. It is He who is our *"hope of glory"* (Col. 1:27) now and eternally. We need not fear His condemnation or that of anyone else. Regardless of our failure or what others think of us, we can turn to Him and revel in His love and acceptance, assured that, as we trust Him and rest in Him, He is seeking to change us into His image *"from glory to glory"* (2 Cor. 3:18), even when it least seems like it.

Do We Have a Role to Play?

Not only does He assure us of our acceptance in Him and of the adequacy of His work on our behalf, but He tells us what to do so that these blessings will be increasingly real in our daily experience. He tells us to put to death the *"old man"* (Rom. 6:6), or the old practices (Rom. 8:13).

Now, we may find that idea so appealing that we rush off in the strength of the flesh to challenge the deeds of the flesh. But stop and read the lengthy Scripture passage that follows. See Christ as your hope and life, your wisdom and knowledge, your all in all. Respond to the appeal to seek Him at the right hand of God in prayer and worship and thanksgiving and praise.

Start spending an increasing amount of time alone with Him, seeking Him for Himself alone, not for any temporal thing. Let Him become increasingly precious to you. Then, throughout the day, whenever you're aware that you're succumbing to life's pressures and are hurried and harried, whenever God has faded into the background and you're excessively conscious of yourself and others, withdraw into the chapel of your heart. Worship Him, and let the cares of this life subside as you return to living at home in God.

Selections from the Book of Colossians

I'd like to share some verses from Colossians that emphasize this idea of being at home in God.

To [His saints] *God willed to make known what are the riches of the glory of this mystery among the Gentiles: which is **Christ in you, the hope of glory**. Him we preach, warning every man and teaching every man in all wisdom, that we may present every man **perfect in Christ Jesus**. To this end I also labor, striving according to His working which works in me mightily....That* [your] *hearts may be encouraged, being knit together in love, and attaining to all riches of the full assurance of understanding, to the knowledge of the mystery of God, both of the Father and of Christ, **in whom** are hidden all the treasures of wisdom and knowledge....As you have therefore received Christ Jesus the Lord, so walk **in Him**, rooted and built up **in Him** and established in the faith, as you have been taught, abounding in it with thanksgiving. Beware lest anyone cheat you through philosophy and empty deceit, according to the tradition of men, according to the basic principles of the world, and not according to Christ. For **in Him** dwells all the fullness of the Godhead bodily; and you are complete **in Him**, who is the head of all principality and power....*[You were] *buried **with Him** in baptism, in which you also were raised **with Him** through faith in the working of God, who raised Him from the dead. And you...He has made alive together **with Him**,* *having forgiven you all trespasses....Having disarmed principalities and powers, He made a public spectacle of them, triumphing over them in it. So let no one judge you in* [certain matters]....*Let no one cheat you of your reward....If then you were raised* **with Christ**, *seek those things which are above, where Christ is, sitting at the right hand of God. Set your mind on things above, not on things on the earth. For you died, and your life is hidden with Christ in God. When Christ who is our life appears, then you also will appear* **with Him** *in glory. Therefore put to death your members which are on the earth....Christ is all and in all....And let the peace of God rule in your hearts, to which also you were called in one body; and be thankful....And whatever you do in word or deed, do all in the name of the Lord Jesus, giving thanks to God the Father through Him....Continue earnestly in prayer, being vigilant in it with thanksgiving.*

(Col. 1:27–29; 2:2–3, 6–10, 12–13, 15–16, 18; 3:1–5, 11, 15, 17; 4:2, emphasis added)

A Thankful Heart

Would you take a good look at that passage again? God—by the terms *God, Christ, Him,* and *He*—is named thirty-one times. And some form of the word *thank* is found four times. Do you suppose that gratitude to the glorious God who is always enough, who is all-sufficient in all things to all men, might be a key factor in your walking with Him in rest, joy, peace, and liberty?

Do you suppose that thanksgiving might be one form of the worship I've so frequently advised you to give God? Could thankfulness of heart be the quiet of heart worship, an "open sesame" to that rest, peace, joy, and liberty in the Lord, in whom *"we live and move and have our being"* (Acts 17:28)? Indeed it is, for as we just read in Colossians, we should

> *Continue earnestly in prayer, being vigilant in it with thanksgiving.* (Col. 4:2)

Conclusion

I'd like to conclude by asking the same question that I asked at the start of this book. Is God big to you, overshadowing all else, or do the problems and difficulties of life overshadow your God? I trust that as you spend more and more time in loving communion with God, He will more and more overshadow all else in your life. I trust that you will truly find God to be your *"all in all"* (1 Cor. 15:28).

Addendum

I've frequently observed that God's timing is meticulous. While writing this book, one morning I typed into my prayer diary most of the following and found it to be a summary of what I've been saying here about how to live happily.

> I'm waking up feeling negative, guilty, unhappy.
> And I'm writing a book on happiness.
> This must not continue.
> Stop it, Lord.
>
> My joy must be in You.
> It can never be in myself.
> Nor can it be in anything I do.
> It must be in You.
> All I can do about it is get to You
> in whatever sense I can get to You.
>
> The less activity I engage in as I get to You,
> the more complete,
> the more satisfying will be my relationship with You.
> Words like *quiet, silent, waiting, resting,*
> *at ease, content, meek, nothing, empty—*
> they all come close to describing this
> "getting to You."

But no words really can describe it.
It's just You. You alone. You ever. You always.
Trusting You with everything may certainly be
a help and an encouragement in getting to You.
So may worshiping You, praising You, honoring You,
uplifting You, exalting You, thanking You,
rejoicing in You, looking to You, coming to You.
So may finding the cause of my grief, repenting of it,
or, if more appropriate, letting it go.
So may slowing down, letting go of all
the have-tos of life.
So may recognizing my place in You,
accepted in the Beloved,
Your righteousness placed to my account,
me blameless in You,
You perfect in me, my very life.

But nothing short of You, Yourself, as my reality,
my environment, my all,
will ultimately satisfy.
To add anything to You is to take something away
from You
and leave me with an incomplete, inadequate God.
This will not do.

There's one way to make certain I can't be happy.
That's to disapprove of something
You permit in my life,
to resist it.
By resisting anything You permit in my life,
no matter how undesirable it may seem,
I resist You.
That's hardly the way to get to You
as I've just described.

214

Instead it drives a wedge between us
and makes me unhappy in a hurry.

Another way to be unhappy is to choose myself in
any sense over You,
to disobey and displease You,
or to give myself unnecessary attention,
robbing You of the attention You alone deserve.

Still another way to be unhappy is
to be hurried and harried,
to have to,
to be pressed and pressured.
Even in prayer I can feel the pressures of have-to.
This mustn't be.
Just to be there with my God is enough.
You must be nothing less than that ever.
ENOUGH!

About the Author

Ron Marr was born in Caledonia, Ontario, Canada, on March 14, 1933, the second youngest of a family of eight children born to Eldon Wray and Clara Muriel Marr, both of largely Scottish ancestry.

Ron's father was found by Christ when Ron was a wide-eyed child. Soon Ron was participating in the excited spiritual conversations of the newly born-again adults that surrounded his father and was "preaching" in "play church."

Ron received Christ as his Savior when he was about nine years old. He graduated from Prairie Bible Institute expecting to serve God on the foreign mission field.

Instead, he directed Youth for Christ ministries in Winnipeg and Montreal from 1955 to 1967. There he enjoyed working with Christian youth, helping many young people find Christ, some entering the ministry in various parts of the world.

In 1957 he married Ruth Peters. She had been born August 5, 1935, into a family of nine children, to Henry Esau and Katherine Schroeder Peters, of Mennonite heritage. Nearly all of the eight who lived to maturity entered the ministry.

In 1960 and 1964, first Sherrie Colleen then Bonnie Lynn were born to Ron and Ruth. Years later, Sherrie married Chris Robins, who now does all the printing for Pastor Marr's ministries while employed full-time in managing a print shop elsewhere. Sherrie writes and sings for Jesus, and she and Chris have two children, Jennifer and Sean. Bonnie's husband is an elementary school principal and Bonnie a teacher who now cares for Ryan, Bethany, and Jordan. Praise God, they all love and serve the Lord.

From 1970 to 1986 Ron edited and published *The Christian Inquirer* newspaper and other publications he founded. He also directed several activist family and freedom organizations that he began. When he was forced financially to discontinue these ministries, they had nearly 100,000 paid subscribers and fifty employees. God used this traumatic situation, along with Ruthie's worsening health, to force Ron to his knees. (Ruthie was diagnosed with Parkinson's Disease in 1970 and demands much of Ron's time night and day in caring for her.) During long hours of prayer, God taught him "a Christianity that really works" and led him to write a book by that title. Whitaker House has printed over 50,000 copies. Hundreds have testified that God has used this book to change their lives. *How to Live Happy and Healthy When Your World Is Falling Apart* is another book recently authored by Ron Marr.

Over the years, Ron has pastored several churches part-time and has been a guest on numerous radio and television programs across the continent.

In 1986 he began WorldWide Revival Prayer Fellowship and later ChristLife, Inc., as agencies through which to minister. They have printed and distributed around the world hundreds of thousands of copies of about eighty messages.

As God provides, a sample pack of these pamphlets will be sent to you free and without obligation upon request. Please see the copyright page for the phone number and address you may use to order these and other valuable resources.

Also by Ron Marr:

A Christianity That Really Works

Learn to live in continuous personal revival through this simply yet beautifully written book.

Testimonials include:

"The best book I've ever read!"

"Turned me around."

"Draws me closer to the Lord."

"Rekindled my spirit."

"Redirected my focus to Christ."

"I read some of it every day."

"Send 50 copies."

"We want a copy for every member of our church."